Redeeming *The Prince*

IL PRINCIPE DI NICCHOLO MACHIA
VELLO AL MAGNIFICO LOREN.
ZO DI PIERO DE MEDICI.

LA VITA DI CASTRVCCIO CASTRA.
CANI DA LVCCA A ZANOBI BVON
DELMONTI ET A LVIGI ALEMAN.
NI DESCRITTA PER IL
MEDESIMO.

IL MODO CHE TENNE IL DVCA VA.
LENTINO PER AMMAZAR VITEL
LOZO, OLIVEROTTO DA FER.
MO IL.S.PAOLO ET IL DV
CA DI GRAVINA ORSI
NI IN SENIGAGLIA,
DESCRITTA PER
IL MEDESIMO.

Con Gratie, & Priuilegi di, N.S. Clemente
VII.& altri Principi, che intra il termino di. X.
Anni non ſi ſtampino, ne ſtampati ſi uendino:
ſotto le pene, che in eſsi ſi contengono.
M. D. XXXII.

Redeeming *The Prince*

THE MEANING OF MACHIAVELLI'S MASTERPIECE

Maurizio Viroli

PRINCETON UNIVERSITY PRESS
Princeton & Oxford

Copyright © 2014 by Princeton University Press

Published by Princeton University Press, 41 William Street,
Princeton, New Jersey 08540

In the United Kingdom: Princeton University Press,
6 Oxford Street, Woodstock, Oxfordshire OX20 1TW

press.princeton.edu

FRONTISPIECE: Title page of Machiavelli's *Il Principe*, 1532.
Rare Books Division, Department of Rare Books and Special
Collection, Princeton University Library.
Photo: Princeton University Library.

Library of Congress Cataloging-in-Publication Data

Viroli, Maurizio.
Redeeming "The prince" : the meaning of Machiavelli's
masterpiece / Maurizio Viroli.
pages cm
Includes bibliographical references and index.
ISBN 978-0-691-16001-6 (hardcover : alk. paper) 1. Machiavelli,
Niccolò, 1469–1527. Principe. 2. POLITICAL SCIENCE /
History & Theory. 3. HISTORY / Europe / Italy. 4. HISTORY /
Modern / 16th Century. 5. PHILOSOPHY / Political. I. Title.

JC143.M3946 V47 2013   2013017926

British Library Cataloging-in-Publication Data is available

This book has been composed in Adobe Caslon Pro

Printed on acid-free paper. ∞

Printed in the United States of America

1 3 5 7 9 10 8 6 4 2

Every day I discover you to be a greater prophet than
the Hebrews or any other nation ever had.

—Filippo Casavecchia to Niccolò Machiavelli
in Pisa or Florence, June 17, 1509

Even as I am writing these words the bells are
ringing far and wide, unceasingly, telling that the
Italians are in Rome: the temporal power is falling,
the people are shouting, "Long live the unity of
Italy!" Let there be glory to Machiavelli!

—Francesco De Sanctis,
Rome, September 20, 1870

CONTENTS

FIGURES

PREFACE

This book originates from a suggestion by Robert Tempio, senior editor at Princeton University Press. It was he who encouraged me to write an essay to elucidate—on the occasion of the 500-year anniversary of its composition—the meaning and value of Machiavelli's *Prince*. I thank him for having persuaded me to embark on a new project. After having worked for some time on Machiavelli's republican ideas, to focus on his allegedly "princely" text has been a fascinating intellectual experience that has led me to assert, as the reader will see, that in fact there is no difference at all between Machiavelli the republican political writer and Machiavelli the advisor of princes.

I have occasionally used here materials that I had previously published in *Machiavelli's God* (2010). The subject and the argument of the two essays are different. I was focusing there on Machiavelli's ideas about God and religion and on their impact on the scholars and the political militants who wrote on the issue of a religious and moral reformation in Italy; here I discuss the intended meaning of Machiavelli's *Prince* and the influence, over the centuries, of his myth of the redeemer and of his ideas on political redemption. Yet, a number of sources and references in *Machiavelli's God* seemed to me necessary and irreplaceable to properly clarify and sustain my argument in *Redeeming "The Prince."*

In this work I have tried to apply a methodological perspective that I had already outlined in another previous work of mine: *As if God Existed: Religion and Liberty in the History of Italy* (2012). I am referring to the idea of examining an author's political writings in connection with the study of his life, in particular his passions, beliefs, and commitments. In the case of Machiavelli's *Prince*, this approach has allowed me to suggest a number of hypotheses concerning the date of composition of the final chapter, the "Exhortation to liberate Italy from the Barbarians," and the meaning of *The Prince*. Readers will judge if my views are convincing, and the method wise. I intend, in future works, to better elucidate and apply the new, or rediscovered, method that I would tentatively call "Ideas and Lives."

My sincere gratitude goes to the colleagues and friends who have discussed with me the argument of this essay, in particular George Kateb and Jean-Jacques Marchand. I have also learned a lot from Quentin Skinner and the other participants in the workshop on "The Meaning of *The Prince*" (February 7–9, 2013) that I have organized with Anthony Grafton under the auspices of The University Centre for Human Values, the Departments of History and Politics, and The Council on Humanities. My thanks go to all these institutions and their directors and chairs. I also wish to express my appreciation to Robert P. George and Bradford Wilson for having organized, under the auspices of the James Madison Programs, a debate with Harvey C. Mansfield in Princeton (December 9, 2012) that has greatly helped me refine my ideas on *The Prince*.

This book will appear a few months after I have become Professor of Politics, Emeritus, at Princeton University. The transition to the emeritus status marks the end of my career as an active professor at Princeton University. In all candour, with no rhetorical embellishment or exaggeration, I wish to assert here that I owe Princeton University the most important intellectual, moral, and personal experience of my entire life. It is a great consolation for me, and an honor, to know that I will carry the title of Professor Emeritus at Princeton University until the end of my days. As I am now serving at the University of Italian Switzerland in Lugano and am about to begin a new chapter at the University of Texas at Austin, I fondly remember the many years that I have spent at Princeton. I arrived in the USA after a rather impressive list of professional humiliations and defeats in the Italian academic world, and I have found in my new country nothing but rewards, respect, and honors. It is with deep conviction that I want to express here my gratitude to the persons that made it all possible, from my arrival at Princeton in 1987. Among them I wish to single out Anna Elisabetta Galeotti and her late husband Franco Ferraresi, Amy Gutmann, George Kateb, Alan Ryan, Ezra Suleiman, Michael Walzer, Diane and William Price, Paul Sigmund, and other friends who are no longer with us, like Stanley Kelley, Walter Murphy, Clifford Geertz, Albert O. Hirschman. A very special thank-you goes to the "brigade" (to use a word dear to Machiavelli) of political theorists now serving at Princeton, to Leslie E. Gerwin and to the other colleagues who have helped me in the transition to the emeritus status. This difficult passage in my life would have been painful without the love and the support of my wife Maria Gabriella Argnani and my daughters Giulia and Simona. I dedicate this book to all the people who have contributed to make it possible for a young (many years ago) scholar with no hopes, born poor in a peripheral street in a small Italian town, to become a professor in one of the most distinguished universities in the world.

Florence, May 12, 2013

Redeeming *The Prince*

Introduction

The majority of scholars have damned Machiavelli's *The Prince* as the work of a teacher of evil. Those few who have written words of praise have interpreted it as the "book of Republicans," to cite Jean-Jacques Rousseau's famous sentence from the *Contrat Social*;[1] or as the text that inaugurates modern political realism and modern political science; or as the courageous essay that at last has explained to us that the actions of princes cannot be judged using the same criteria that we use for human actions in general and that therefore politics is autonomous from ethics.

In my opinion, none of these defenses of Machiavelli is valid. The view that *The Prince* is the "book of Republicans" comes from Rousseau's desire to rescue its author's bad reputation and make *The Prince* consistent with the *Discourses on Livy*, the text in which Machiavelli developed a comprehensive republican theory of liberty and government. Although the intention was noble, this claim misrepresents the meaning of the text. Machiavelli did not intend to reveal to the people the princes' vices and incite in them antimonarchical sentiments. Republicans can surely learn from *The Prince* precious pieces of political wisdom, but there is no question that Machiavelli's text is neither a satire of the prince nor does it embody any sort of oblique or cryptic message. He seriously wanted to instruct a new prince, a special sort of new prince, as I shall explain later.

The view that we owe Machiavelli credit for the discovery of the principle of the "autonomy of politics from morals," though advanced by illustrious scholars, is also indefensible for two main reasons: first because it distorts Machiavelli's text, and second because it is philosophically very weak.[2] The passages that the supporters of the theory of the autonomy of politics cite are taken from chapters XV, XVI, XVII, and XVIII of *The Prince*, which form a well-identifiable section of the work. In these chapters, Machiavelli makes the infamous, or famous, assertion that it is necessary for a new prince to learn not to be good and to be able to enter into evil, if necessary. The problem with citing these passages as the foundation of the autonomy of politics is that Machiavelli here is referring not only to princes but to all human beings. The title of chapter XV, which opens the entire discussion of politics and morals is "Of Those Things for Which Men, and Particularly Princes, Are Praised or Blamed." The conclusion, at the end of chapter XVIII, concerns all human beings: "and in the actions of *all* men, and especially of princes, where there is no tribunal to which to appeal, one must consider the final result."[3]

One might claim that Machiavelli here is rejecting the relevance of ethics for all human beings, but not that he asserts that there are rules to judge princes and rules to judge ordinary human beings. To believe that Machiavelli advocated such a principle would mean attributing to him the idea that a prince acts according to the rules of politics when, to found and preserve a state, he perpetrates a cruelty, while he violates those same rules if he attains the same result by being humane. In addition to being sheer nonsense, there is no trace of such an assertion in Machiavelli's writings. Had Machiavelli truly theorized the principle of the autonomy of politics, on the other hand, he would have forged a very poor concept. The actions of politicians *are* judged, and *must* be judged on the basis of ethical standards. If not, we would have no defense against corrupt and oppressive politicians.

The argument that the perennial value of Machiavelli's *Prince* consists in the fact that it has inaugurated modern political realism is open to serious objections. Machiavelli was a realist *sui generis* who was not solely interested in describing, interpreting, or explaining political facts but liked to imagine political realities very different from the existing one. In the *Discourses on Livy*, he conceived a rebirth of ancient Roman political wisdom; in the *Art of War*, he fantasized about the restoration of Roman military orders and virtue. If we want to see a true realist, we must read Guicciardini, not Machiavelli. And Guicciardini considered Machiavelli a fine political expert, but one too keen to rely on the examples of the past and not sufficiently attentive to the specific features of political life.

What then is *The Prince* about, and what is its lasting value, if any? My answer is that Niccolò Machiavelli wrote *The Prince* to design and invoke a redeemer of Italy capable of creating, with God's help, new and good political order, thereby attaining perennial glory. The theory, and the myth, of the redeemer is, in my opinion, the enduring value of Machiavelli's little book. As I shall document in the last chapter of this essay, the interpretation of *The Prince* as a discourse on political redemption has a long and fascinating history. Yet contemporary scholarship, with a few exceptions, has instead disregarded or dismissed it.[4]

The influential scholar Leo Strauss, for instance, in his essay from 1957, asserted that *The Prince* is a scientific book "because it conveys a general teaching that is based on reasoning"; at the same time, he maintains, it is the opposite of a scientific or detached work precisely because it "culminates in a passionate call to action—in a call addressed to a contemporary Italian prince." The book begins with a very dry assertion and closes with "a highly rhetorical last chapter which ends in a quotation from a patriotic poem in Italian." In this work, Machiavelli is both an investigator or a teacher and an advisor, "if not a preacher." We must recognize *The Prince* as a book "with a traditional surface with a revolutionary center ." Revolutionary in the precise sense of "a man who breaks the law, the laws as a whole, in order to replace it by a new law which he believes to be better than the old law."[5]

Strauss claims that the last chapter is the "natural conclusion of the book" and as such is the key to understand the whole text.[6] He also maintains that the "Exhortation" is not "a piece of mere rhetoric," and utterly rejects the view that Machiavelli "was not capable of thinking clearly and writing with consummate skill," when he composed those pages. But as a piece of specific counsel addressed to a specific new prince, Lorenzo de' Medici, the "Exhortation" is seriously lacking, because, Strauss explains, "it is silent about the difficulties in the way." The chapter creates the impression that the only thing required for the liberation of Italy is the Italians' strong loathing of foreign domination and their ancient valor; the liberator of Italy can expect spontaneous cooperation from all his patriots and he can be sure that they will fly to take up arms against the foreigners once he "takes the banner."

The problem with Strauss's view, and that of many others, is, as I will illustrate here, that the "Exhortation" *is* a fine piece of political rhetoric that ends an oration whose purpose is to impel action. As such, it is perfect—nothing is missing. To motivate a new prince to be a redeemer, Machiavelli must depict the whole enterprise as not only possible but also easy and must promise the greatest possible rewards. Machiavelli needed a political myth, but myths, to work, cannot be presented in the form of detailed prescriptions for political action.

Strauss also stresses that the "Exhortation" is the key to understanding Machiavelli's pieces of advice on political ethics. The general teachings that Machiavelli offers in the central chapters of *The Prince*, however novel and repulsive, "might seem to be redeemed if it leads up to a particular counsel so respectable, honorable and praiseworthy as that of liberating Italy." The liberation of Italy from the barbarians "means a complete revolution. It requires first and above everything a revolution in thinking about right and wrong. Italians have to learn that the patriotic end hallows every means however much condemned by the most exalted traditions both philosophical and religious."[7]

Strauss understands well the religious tones of Machiavelli's exhortation: "he mentions God as often there as in all other chapters of *The Prince* taken together. He calls the liberator of Italy an Italian 'spirit'; he describes the liberation of Italy as a divine redemption and he suggests its resemblance to the resurrection of the dead as depicted by Ezekiel; he alludes to the miracles wrought by God in Italy." After these acknowledgments, Strauss's tone turns sarcastic: "However much we might wish to be moved by these expressions of religious sentiment, we fail in our effort."[8] The reason Strauss finds Machiavelli's pages unmoving is that he believes that what Machiavelli means by God is nothing but chance. Strauss's essay has in sum the virtue of pointing to the "Exhortation" as the key to understanding *The Prince*, but he soon veers off the right track. Instead of seeing the emancipating content of Machiavelli's text, he proceeds to damn its malignantly concealed immorality.

The seminal essay by Hans Baron, published in 1961, also indicates national redemption as a fundamental theme of Machiavelli's *Prince*. Baron claims that *The Prince* was the outcome of the new personal and intellectual experience that Machiavelli lived in the forced solitude of Sant'Andrea in Percussina in the second half of 1513.[9] In addition to his fresh reflections on classical works, Machiavelli used his expertise on "the diplomatic techniques and administrative efficiency that he had learned in the service of the republic" to build up "the rule of a new prince." Machiavelli's key motivation and inspiration for *The Prince*, Baron stresses, was "both his burning desire for a place of action in the world of politics and his wounded Italian feelings," which "caused him to nurture a fresh hope for a powerful founder of a new state."[10] He also tells us that the founder that Machiavelli portrays in *The Prince* is quite different from those he indicates as examples in the *Discourses*, thereby stressing once again the differences separating Machiavelli's two works.[11] Yet Baron does not believe it relevant to go beyond this general, though precious, indication. Of the final

"Exhortation," he mentions only that "the sincerity of Machiavelli's call, in the epilogue of the *Prince*, for a deliverer of Italy from foreign domination has remained a matter of debate until today." He did not consider it necessary to explain how in fact Machiavelli's hope for the new founder in 1513 translated into the text of *The Prince*.

Some years later, in two papers of 1968 and 1972, Baron reexamined the issue of the date of composition of chapter XXVI, and discussed whether we should regard the conclusion of *The Prince* as the key political message to which the entire work was oriented since the beginning. On close examination of the Italian political context of the period from late 1513 to October 1516, Baron reaches the conclusion that

> another incubus of Machiavellian scholarship, has been removed: the "national" interpretation of the *Prince*, created by Hegel, Fichte and Ranke, and the Italian historians of the *Risorgimento*, and still maintained by Meinecke and Chabod, will never have the power to make a comeback. We can now grasp, unconcerned, the pragmatic character of the *Prince* and appraise it realistically. We are at liberty to draw the picture of the evolution of Machiavelli from the Machiavellianism of the *Prince* to the new historical vision and the republican and moral values of the *Discourses*.[12]

Also the scholars who have made fundamental contributions to the study of *The Prince* by placing it in the context of the humanist advice for princes books did not focus, in general, on the "Exhortation." Felix Gilbert, in his

article of 1939, "The Humanist Concept of the Prince and
The Prince of Machiavelli," does not even touch the issue.
In a later essay, "The Concept of Nationalism in Machiavelli's *Prince*" (1954), Gilbert concentrates his attention on
the last chapter and mentions the debate that had been
going on for years between the advocates of the view that
the "Exhortation" is a mere rhetorical peroration contrasting the pragmatic style of the rest of the book and those
who maintain that it was instead the core of Machiavelli's
text. Gilbert prefers to analyze the "Exhortation" from a
different angle—namely, to see how it related to early-
sixteenth-century ideological and political views on Italy's
liberation. What makes Machiavelli's "Exhortation" truly
unique, Gilbert concludes, is his recommendation, against
the Florentine aristocracy, to carry out the policy of Italian
redemption "over the head of the individual state, relying
on the feelings of the masses," rather than on the cooperation among states. Though Gilbert left in the background
the issue of the relevance of the "Exhortation" for the understanding of *The Prince*, he surely succeeded in isolating
its powerful and subversive message of emancipation.

In 1978, Quentin Skinner, in his groundbreaking *Foundations of Modern Political Thought*, proposed another reading of *The Prince* within the context of Italian humanism.[13]
Contrary to the view that *The Prince* is a book *sui generis*,
Skinner argues that it is in fact a "recognizable contribution"
to the genre of advice books for princes and at the same
time a radical critique of them. The revolutionary meaning of Machiavelli's little work therefore lies in his direct
attack on the humanist and Christian tenet that a prince,
if he wishes to preserve his state and attain perennial glory,

must at all times follow the political virtues of justice, magnanimity, fortitude, prudence, and temperance, as well as the distinctively princely virtues of clemency, liberality, and honesty. To be a truly virtuous prince for Machiavelli meant instead to adapt one's own behavior and political strategy to the changing winds of fortune and to display outstanding military ability in raising and commanding loyal troops. In Skinner's perspective, the "Exhortation"—in which Machiavelli also dishonors himself in an "uncharacteristic moment of flattery"—is one of the sections of the work that illuminates Machiavelli's concern for the paramount role of virtue, properly redefined, in political affairs. As Skinner has clarified in a more recent study, "the prince's basic aim, we learn in a phrase that echoes throughout *Il Principe*, must be *mantenere lo stato*, to maintain his power and existing frame of government." It must also be "to establish such a form of government as will bring honor to himself and benefit the whole body of subjects."[14]

In my view, the "Exhortation" is particularly relevant precisely for its role in the assessment of Machiavelli's work in the context of advice books for princes. No other text of this genre ends like *The Prince*. Petrarch brings to a close his letter to Francis of Carrara with an appeal to correct "the morals" of the subjects of Padua. One moral that stands in urgent need of correction is the practice of loud and indecent wailing in the streets and churches upon someone's death. Such a habit, Petrarch, stresses, is "contrary to any decent and moral behavior and unworthy of any city under your rule." "You must therefore immediately command," Petrarch enjoins, that "wailing women should not be permitted to step outside their homes."[15]

Bartolomeo Sacchi's (Platina) *De Principe* (around 1470) ends soberly with a chapter on war instruments apt to ensure the prince a blessed and felicitous victory.[16] Giovanni Pontano's *De Principe* (1468) closes with a long discussion on the fundamental princely virtue of majesty in which he details how a fine prince ought to speak, dress, walk, eat, and so on. His final words are a profession of modesty: "you shall read my work not to learn something, since there is nothing for you to learn, but only to be able to recognize yourself and what you already are doing with universal praise in the pursuit of glory."[17]

Francesco Patrizi dedicates the last pages of his *De Regno* to instruct the king how he ought to live the last day of his life. The king's main concern, he remarks, is to have an honest death, and not to worry about the sepulchre, because if he has lived according to virtue, he will be forever praised.[18] As Quentin Skinner has clarified, *The Prince* is surely a subversive critique of the accepted wisdom on princely virtues, but it is no less true that it also contains an equally radical critique of the parochialism and lack of true greatness of the princes of his time and of their learned humanist mentors.

In his highly influential book *The Machiavellian Moment* (1975), John G. A. Pocock eloquently claims that *The Prince* is "an analytic study of innovation and its consequences" in which Machiavelli focuses his attention on the ultimate political problem of his time—that is, the "problem of *fortuna*."[19] What we find in Machiavelli's most famous work, Pocock maintains, is "a typology of innovators and their relations with *fortuna*." Innovation simply means that the new prince has overthrown or replaced some form of government that preceded him. The title of the treatise is itself misleading, because as we advance in our reading, it appears evident that the category of the "innovator" has replaced the category of the "new prince," in the sense that the former "is more comprehensive and capable of greater theoretical precision than the latter.[20] Yet, Pocock does not consider the final exhortation, in which Machiavelli delineates the image of the liberating hero, as the point of arrival toward which all previous chapters "are to be seen as leading up to."[21] In his view, Machiavelli does not present here "a single rounded portrait, but a gallery of specimen types of innovators."[22] As a result, *The Prince* is for Pocock an essay on political innovation in general in its relationship with *fortuna*, not an essay on political redemption specifically conceived against foreign domination.

Political theorists of the early 1960s, who composed excellent works on radical and revolutionary political theory and political practices, also did not regard, in general, Machiavelli's *Prince* as a text that contains a genuine or particularly relevant liberation message. Sheldon Wolin, in his *Politics and Vision: Continuity and Innovation in Western Political Thought* (1960), presents *The Prince* as a text that rejects traditional norms like natural law and is exclusively focused on "questions of power."[23] Machiavelli openly showed his antipathy toward hereditary monarchies, and the new man he painted was "the political arriviste," a figure that was to bedevil modern politics. His creed was the maxim "I love my patria more than my soul," and when he was writing on national revival, Wolin notes, Machiavelli displayed "an important substratum of religious feelings and imagery." But the focus of his *Prince* is power, not emancipation. Machiavelli considers the State as an "aggregate of power," and the new kind of political action he encourages ought to be above all "an economy of violence, a science of controlled application of force."[24]

For Hannah Arendt, Machiavelli is "the spiritual father of revolution in the modern sense" because he possesses "that conscious and passionate yearning to revive the spirit and the institution of Roman antiquity which later became so characteristic of the political thought of the eighteenth century."[25] The protagonists of the revolutionary experiments justified and supported revolution as a return to the true principles of the political community. Great modern revolutions originated as "restorations or renewals" in the Machiavellian meaning of renovations that return the body politic to its origins and thus save it from corruption and death. Machiavelli's idea of the rebirth of the ideals and virtues of antiquity had a very powerful influence, as Arendt points out, in the thought of the founders of the American republic:

> From a historical point of view, it was as if the rebirth of antiquity that had taken place during the Renaissance, and had come to a sudden end with the advent of the modern age, had suddenly found a new lease on life; as if the republican fervor of the Italian city-states in their brief existence—already condemned, as Machiavelli knew full well, by the advent of the nation-state—had only be sleeping, so that it could give the nations of Europe the time to grow, as it were, under the tutelage of absolute monarchs and enlightened despots.[26]

Machiavelli contributed to revolutionary theory precisely with his thoughts on the role of religion in the foundation of new political orders. The birth of a new political order, in fact, demands, alongside violence, religion; alongside power, authority—the force of arms and the force of words. "Machiavelli," concludes Arendt, "the sworn enemy of religious considerations in political affairs, was driven to ask for divine assistance and even inspiration in legislators—just like the 'enlightened' men of the eighteenth century, John Adams and Robespierre for example."[27] Arendt is right to stress that the founding fathers of the American Revolution made wise use of Machiavelli's ideas—however indirectly received—on the renewal and rebirth of political bodies. But she has always in mind the *Discourses on Livy*, not *The Prince*. Modern revolutionary political thought and practices, in her view, did not recognize *The Prince* among its sources.

One of the best works on the origin of modern radical politics, Michael Walzer's *Revolution of the Saints*, fails to notice the redeeming message of Machiavelli's *Prince*. Walzer considers Machiavelli the advocate of a form of political action that discourages the citizens' conscious engagement and therefore lacks any liberating value:

> In the early sixteenth century, Machiavelli's *Discourses* offer an imaginative and realistic discussion of political life and are filled with a genuine yearning for civic virtue and citizenship. His *Prince*, however, is not a program for activist citizens, but a handbook for adventurers. The new consciousness of politics as a matter of individual skill and calculation, which Machiavelli best embodies, was as yet unaccompanied by a new ideology that might give form to the creative work, limiting and shaping the

ambition of princes and making available to them the
willing cooperation of other men. The new consciousness thus produced only an intensely personal, faction-
ridden politics. Artistry freed from form gave rise to the
political *condottiere*, the virtuoso of power.[28]

Even if English seventeenth-century puritan militants
were following Machiavelli's "rational, amoral, pragmatic
consideration of political methods," *The Prince* is for Walzer one of the last voices of the old medieval politics, not
one of the first instances of modern radical politics marked
by the continuous involvement of men "systematically active, imaginatively responsive to opportunity, seeking victory" sustained by the persuasion that their struggle against
tyranny was consistent with God's plans.[29]

A text like *The Prince*, in which the author extols Moses,
Romulus, Cyrus, and Theseus as the exemplary figures that
a new prince should imitate, hardly qualifies as a handbook
for political adventurers. Equally incorrect is the view that
Machiavelli's conception of political emancipation discourages active citizenship. In the "Exhortation," Machiavelli
asserts that a new prince committed to the task of emancipating Italy from foreign domination would surely animate
in the people a widespread devotion and love, and a strong
willingness to serve and fight in the new army created and
commanded by the prince himself.

The model that Machiavelli outlines in the "Exhortation" shows some features of millenarianism. He presents
Italy's emancipation as a swift realization. But he also
largely draws from the biblical Exodus: a people capable
of achieving their own emancipation, through their own

efforts and sufferings, under the guidance of a great political founder not only sent by God but also a friend of God, just like Moses. The Machiavellian founder, and the people devoutly following him, are instruments of God, just like the puritan militants. The glory that they gain, if they succeed in their effort of founding new and good political orders, goes also to the God who has inspired and helped their struggle. If the exodus is the paradigm of radical emancipatory politics, then Machiavelli's *Prince* is surely a book on political emancipation, not a handbook for adventurers.

My interpretation rests on the idea that Machiavelli composed the "Exhortation to liberate Italy," where he openly expresses the *Prince*'s message of emancipation at the time when he wrote the other chapters of his work, between August 1513 and January 1514, not two or three years later, as some scholars have claimed. I discuss the much debated and still unsettled issue of the date of composition of *The Prince* in the first chapter of this essay.

To support my position, I cite internal textual evidence as well as references to external political events. I also consider, at some length, what kind of man Niccolò Machiavelli was when he sat down to write his *Prince*. I am neither attempting to produce a psychological study nor suggesting some kind of causal connection between Machiavelli's existential condition and the text. More modestly, I claim that the study of Machiavelli's life—in particular, the interpretation of his passions and beliefs—helps us to understand the meaning of *The Prince* and to better identify the date of composition of the "Exhortation."[30] Machiavelli's private letters do in fact indicate that between early 1514 and late 1517 he was too disconsolate and miserable to write a text like the "Exhortation" to invoke a redeemer of Italy after December 1513 or early 1514. They also allow us to see that Machiavelli imagined Italy's political redemption as strictly intertwined with his own resurrection—that is, the possibility of being himself again, of being able to actively translate his deepest passion, love of country, into political action.

A powerful objection stands against my interpretation, however—that is, that Machiavelli called his work *De Principatibus*, not *De principe*, to suggest that the focus of his discussion is the different types of principalities and how they can be preserved and how they are lost, not the figure of the prince. A possible reply is that in the *Discourses on Livy* (III, 42), Machiavelli refers to his essay as *De Principe*. This change of language could indicate that the essay has evolved from a study of principalities into a study of the prince, or that Machiavelli, a few years after its composition, remembers his essay as being on the prince. On balance, I think that the reasons that support the view that *The Prince* is about the prince as a redeemer and founder are stronger than the reasons that militate in favor of the view that the *Prince* is about principalities.

Can we believe that an author who openly declares that his intention in writing *The Prince* is to concentrate only on the effectual truth of the matter could have composed an essay to design an ideal figure, and to propose a political myth? My reply, in chapter 2, is that Machiavelli was a realist *sui generis* who was not solely interested in describing, interpreting, or explaining political facts but also liked to imagine political realities very different from the existing one and wrote the *Prince*, and all his works, to make the imagined realities he loved real.

My claim that Machiavelli has put the political and moral message he really wanted to convey in the final "Exhortation" receives further and important support from a correct interpretation of the style of *The Prince*. As I will detail in chapter 3, *The Prince* is an oration, in the proper sense of the word, from the first line to the last. This means that Machiavelli has put the most important message, the most important message for him, at the end. And at the end of *The Prince*, we find the "Exhortation," with the myth of the redeemer.

If we read the *Prince* from the angle of the redeemer, we understand better Machiavelli's hotly debated arguments on ethics and politics. As is well known, Machiavelli asserts that "it is necessary for a prince who wants to maintain his state to learn how not to be good, and to use this knowledge or not to use it according to necessity," and that

> a prince, and especially a new prince cannot observe all those things for which men are considered good, for in order to maintain the state, he is often obliged to act against his promise, against charity, against humanity, against religion. And therefore, it is necessary that he have a mind ready to turn itself according to the way the winds of fortune and the changeability of affairs require him; and, as I said above, as long as it is possible he should not deviate from the good, but he should know how to enter into evil when necessity commends it.

He assures us, in chapter VIII, that if new princes resort to "well used" cruelty, they can "remedy their condition with God and with men." He also explains, in the "Exhortation," that the redeemers can count on God's friendship because their enterprise is just: "for their enterprises were no more just, nor easier, nor was God more a friend to them than to you." Machiavelli here explicitly alludes to Moses and the book of Exodus. To have God as friend means not only that the redeemer can count on His help when he has to face almost impossible tasks, but also that God will understand and excuse him if, forced by necessity, he has to enter in evil and not be good. Friends are indulgent. In the Bible, God remains a friend to Moses even after he committed horrible cruelties. What Machiavelli is therefore telling his readers is not that politics is autonomous from ethics but that the redeemer, because of the moral excellence of his task, deserves special consideration.

The much debated issue of the intellectual and political compatibility of *The Prince*—a text in which he teaches a new prince how to conquer and maintain his power—and the *Discourses on Livy*—the acclaimed foundation of modern republican thought—is seen in a new light if we read *The Prince* as an oration on the founder and the redeemer. The prince of *The Prince* is not the founder of a reigning dynasty but the founder of an independent state with good armies and good laws that may evolve, and that Machiavelli would like to see evolving, in a republic. There is no hint in the entire work about rules or criteria of succession. This silence is quite resounding, particularly if we compare Machiavelli's *Prince* with the other advice books for princes that do indeed contain indications on the designation of the successor.

The figure of the founder who acts as a monarch but then opens the path for a republic appears also in other works of Machiavelli. The obvious reference is *Discourses on Livy*, I, 9, where Romulus, who is also one of the heroes of *The Prince*, was surely a king, but the political orders he instituted in Rome were more congenial to a free and civil way of living rather than to a tyranny. When Rome became a republic, very small institutional changes were needed.[31] Another less known example is from the *Discourse on Remodeling the State of Florence* composed in 1520 at Cardinal Giulio de' Medici's request, for Pope Leo X. In that essay, Machiavelli exalts the figure of the reformer of political orders with words very similar to those he had used in *The Prince*, and openly says that as long as the pope and the cardinal are alive, their power will be a monarchy ("ella è una monarchia"). Afterward, Florence must resume its republican institutions.[32]

A founder and a redeemer are necessary for both republics and kingdoms. In both cases, they must have extraordinary authority, display exactly the same virtues, and face the necessity of entering in evil. Machiavelli's *Prince* is indeed the "book of Republicans." Not in the sense that it reveals the horrible vices of the prince and instills in its readers a hatred for monarchy, as Rousseau believed, but in the sense that it delineates the image of the founder and redeemer that republican political theory needs. After all, Machiavelli explicitly tells us that, "If princes are superior to peoples in ordering laws, forming civil lives, and ordering new statutes and orders, peoples are so much superior in maintaining things ordered that without doubt they attain the glory of those who order them."[33] Unless we are prepared to believe that good republics come into existence, endure, and are reformed only through the wisdom and the active participation of their citizens, we must accept the view that republics need great political leaders. *The Prince* is about great political leadership, the leadership of founders and redeemers. Hence, it is not a problematic alternative to the *Discourses*, but an integral counterpoint to it. Together, they make for a fine theory of political emancipation.

It is just speculation, but I believe that *The Prince* has remained relevant for five hundred years, and will probably survive in good health for many years to come, because it is a living work, as Antonio Gramsci nicely put it.[34] It is a living work in the sense that Machiavelli was able to infuse in that text a poignant message that has helped to stimulate political action with redemptive goals, be they national, social, or inspired by ideals of republican liberty.

In history, resurrections and redemptions are rare experiences. As hopes and aspirations in the lives of peoples, they are, however, real and long-lasting. Readers perceive that while Machiavelli was writing about an imagined redeemer of Italy, he was striving for his own resurrection. As he was composing the pages of *The Prince*, he was no longer a defeated man, deeply wounded in his body and his soul, compelled to live his days as "Quondam Secretario" (former Secretary). He was again himself, a man who found in grand politics his spiritual nourishment. And for him, grand politics *was* the politics of founders and redeemers. What makes *The Prince* exceptional is that it is a text on political redemption and founding composed by a man who was trying to redeem himself. This is not the only meaning to be found in *The Prince*. Only the theme of redemption and founding, however, casts the proper light on all the pages of Machiavelli's oration and permits us to savor its dramatic beauty.

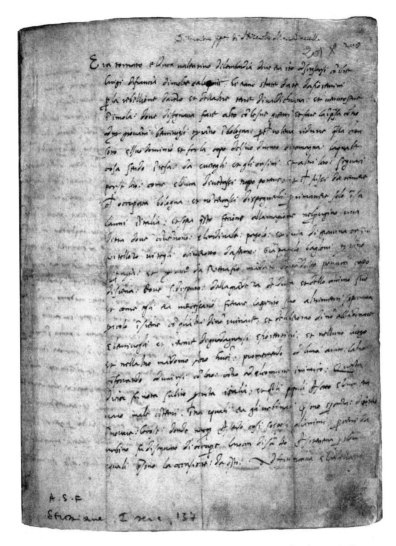

Figure 1. Carte Strozziane I 137, c. 201. Courtesy Archivio di Stato Firenze. Page showing Machiavelli's handwriting and signature.

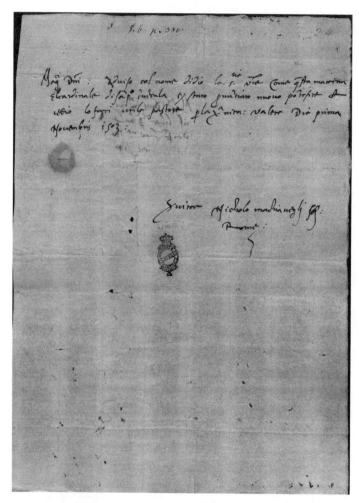

Figure 2. Machiavelli Papers, I C. 24r. Courtesy Biblioteca Nazionale
Centrale di Firenze. Page showing Machiavelli's handwriting
and signature.

CHAPTER ONE

The Prince as a Redeemer

The Main Idea

The redeemer appears in the *Prince*, along with the armed prophet, in chapter VI ("Of new principalities acquired by one's own troops and virtue"). Until then, Machiavelli had discussed, in a cold and detached tone, the various types of principalities—new, hereditary, mixed—and had isolated one of the general principles of his work: "I say, therefore, that in completely new principalities, where there is a new prince, greater or lesser difficulty in maintaining them exists according to the greater or lesser virtue of the person who acquires them." Then he cites the great men who became princes by their own virtue and armies and not because of Fortune. The first in his list is Moses, whom he presents as a prophet: "Although we should not discuss Moses, since he was a mere executor of things he was ordered to do by God, nevertheless he must be admired at least for the grace that made him worthy of speaking with God." Thanks to God's grace, and his own virtue, Moses is the forerunner for the other most excellent men: the methods used by other founders—Cyrus, Romulus, and Theseus—were not that different from those of Moses who had God as a teacher.[1]

Machiavelli also anticipates in chapter VI the argument that he will expand in the "Exhortation"—namely, that Fortune offers great founders an opportunity to show their outstanding virtue and to accomplish grand political deeds:

> In examining their deeds and their lives, one can see that they received nothing from Fortune except opportunity, which gave them the material they could mould into whatever form they liked. Without that opportunity [*occasione*] the strength of their spirit would have been exhausted, and without that strength, their opportunity would have come in vain. It was therefore necessary for Moses to find the people of Israel slaves in Egypt and oppressed by the Egyptians, in order that they might be disposed to follow him to escape this servitude. It was necessary for Romulus not to stay in Alba, and that he be exposed at birth, so that he might become King of Rome and founder of that nation. It was necessary for Cyrus to find the Persians unhappy about the rule of the Medes, and the Medes rendered soft and effeminate after a lengthy peace. Theseus could not have demonstrated his ability if he had not found the Athenians dispersed. These opportunities, therefore, made these men successful, and their outstanding virtue enabled them to recognize that opportunity, whereby their nation was ennobled and became extremely happy.

Machiavelli introduces the prophet and the founder abruptly, almost as if he intended to astonish the reader.

The first step of his argument is to explain how difficult the foundation of new political orders is:

> Those who, like these men, become princes through their virtue acquire the principality with difficulty, but they hold on to it easily. The difficulties they encounter in acquiring the principality grow, in part out of the new institutions and methods they are forced to introduce in order to establish their state and their security. One should bear in mind that there is nothing more difficult to execute, nor more dubious of success, nor more dangerous to administer, than to introduce new political orders. For the one who introduces them has as his enemies all those who profit from the old order, and he has only lukewarm defenders in all those who might profit from the new order.

Then Machiavelli focuses again on the prophet to highlight the impossibility of succeeding in the work of founding new political orders by the sole power of prophecy—that is, the power of persuasion sustained by an alleged divine inspiration:

> However, if we desire to examine this argument thoroughly, it is necessary to consider whether these innovators act on their own or are dependent on others: that is, if they are forced to beg for help or are able to employ force in conducting their affairs. In the first case, they always come to a bad end and never accomplish anything. But when they depend on their own resources and can

use force, then only seldom do they run the risk of grave danger.

The conclusion of the argument is that a successful founder and redeemer must be an armed prophet:

> From this comes the fact that all armed prophets were victorious and the unarmed came to ruin. For, besides what has been said, people are fickle by nature: it is easy to convince them of something, but difficult to hold them in that conviction. Therefore, affairs should be managed in such a way that when they no longer believe, they can be made to believe by force. Moses, Cyrus, Theseus and Romulus could not have made their institutions respected for long if they had been unarmed; as in our times happened to Brother Girolamo Savonarola, who was ruined in his new institutions when the populace began to believe in them no longer, since he had no way of holding steady those who had believed, nor of making the unbelievers believe."

At the very outset of the essay, the new prince then merges with the prophet and the founder.

To be sure that the reader gets the message that *The Prince* is about the great deeds of armed prophets, Machiavelli sets them as the examples to be followed:

> No one should wonder if, in speaking of principalities that are completely new as to their ruler and form of government, I cite *the greatest examples* [*grandissimi esempli*]. Since men almost always follow the paths trod

Figure 3. Michelangelo Buonarroti, *Moses*, from the tomb of Pope Julius II. Marmo Basilica di San Pietro in Vincoli, Rome, Italy. Photo: Scala / Art Resource, NY.

Figure 4. Fresco of Theseus the Liberator. Museo Archeologico Nazionale, Naples, Italy. Photo: Scala / Art Resource, NY.

by others, and proceed in their affairs by imitation, although they are not fully able to stay on the path of others, nor to equal the virtue of those they imitate, a wise
man should always enter those paths trodden by *great
men* [*uomini grandi*], and imitate those who have been

the most excellent [*quegli che sono stati eccellentissimi imi-tare*], so that if one's own virtue does not match theirs, at least it will have the smell of it [italics mine].

Machiavelli also explicitly directs the reader's attention to the examples of grand political action in the dedicatory letter to Lorenzo di Piero de' Medici that he had originally composed for Giuliano di Lorenzo de' Medici:

> Wishing, therefore, to offer myself to Your Magnificence with some evidence of my devotion to you, I have not found among my belongings anything that I might value more or prize so much as the knowledge of *the deeds of great men* that I have learned from a long experience in modern and a continuous study of antiquity affairs. Having with great care and for a long time thought about and examined *these deeds* and having now set *them* down in a little book, I am sending them to Your Magnificence [italics mine].

An even more precious indication that the prophet and the redeemer are the core of his reflections comes from the famous letter to Vettori of December 10, 1513. He writes in fact:

> When the evening comes, I return home and enter my study; on the threshold I take off my workday clothes, covered with mud and dirt, and put on garments of court and palace. Fitted out appropriately, I step inside the venerable courts of the ancients, where solicitously received by them, I nourish myself on that food that alone is mine and for which I was born; where I am unashamed to

Figure 5. *Lorenzo de' Medici, Duke of Urbino*, 1586, wood, 140 × 116
cm. Inv. 2224. Uffizi, Florence, Italy. Photo: Erich Lessing /
Art Resource, NY. Lorenzo was the dedicatee of *The Prince*.

converse with them and to question them about the motives for their actions.

The Prince, Machiavelli tells us here, is the result of his reflections on the actions of the great men of antiquity ("loro azioni"). The list of their names includes a fair number of princes, captains, and emperors, but the most prominent names are surely those he mentions in chapter VI: Moses, Romulus, Cyrus, and Theseus. Those men are the founders and the redeemers who have attained immortality through their extraordinary virtue, and because they are immortal, they can answer Machiavelli's questions on their actions. The essence of that quite special conversation is distilled in *The Prince*.

As he openly declares, the "Exhortation" is the conclusion of the reflections he has developed throughout *The Prince*:

> Having carefully considered the subject of the above discourses, and wondering within myself whether the present times were propitious to a new prince, and whether there were the elements that would give an opportunity to a wise and virtuous one to introduce a new order of things which would do honor to him and good to the people of this country, it appears to me that so many things concur to favor a new prince that I never knew a time more fit than the present.

He then rephrases the theme of the occasion offered by fortune to a great redeemer:

> And if, as I said, it was necessary that the people of Israel should be captive so as to make manifest the ability

of Moses; that the Persians should be oppressed by the Medes so as to discover the greatness of the soul of Cyrus; and that the Athenians should be dispersed to illustrate the capabilities of Theseus: then at the present time, in order to discover the virtue of an Italian spirit, it was necessary that Italy should be reduced to the extremity she is now in, that she should be more enslaved than the Hebrews, more oppressed than the Persians, more scattered than the Athenians; without head, without order, beaten, despoiled, torn, overrun; and to have endured every kind of desolation."

Having outlined the nature of the occasion that fortune has set up, Machiavelli designs with great eloquence the figure of the redeemer as an armed prophet that he had sketched in chapter VI, as we have seen. He stresses, first, that Italy's emancipation is ordained by God, even if no one has yet been able to carry out God's plan:

And even though, before now, some glimmer of light may have shown itself in a single individual, so that it was possible to believe that God had ordained him for Italy's redemption, yet it was seen how, at the height of his deeds, he was rejected by Fortune, so that Italy, left as without life, waits for him who shall yet heal her wounds and put an end to the ravaging and plundering of Lombardy, to the swindling and taxing of the kingdom and of Tuscany, and cleanse those sores that for long have festered. It is seen how she entreats God to send someone who shall deliver her from these wrongs and barbarous insolences. It is seen also that she is ready and willing to follow a banner if only someone will raise it.

Then, speaking as if he were a prophet, he openly promises God's help: "Although those men were rare and marvelous, they were nevertheless men, and each of them had poorer opportunities than are offered now: for their undertakings were no more just, nor easier than this one, nor was God more a friend to them than to you." As we already know from chapter VI, however, the redeemer must count on an excellent army completely loyal to him:

> To follow these excellent men who redeemed their countries, it is necessary before all else, and as a true basis for every enterprise, to provide yourself with your own soldiers. Although each one of them may be good individually, united together they will become even better, when they see themselves commanded, honoured and well treated by their own prince.

The distinctive quality of the armed prophet is greatness. Leaving aside the reference to the "friendships acquired by a price and not by greatness and nobility of spirit," which I will discuss later, Machiavelli speaks of great deeds in the first paragraph of the famous, or infamous, chapter XVIII ("How a prince should keep his word"). He writes:

> How praise worthy is it for a prince to keep his word and to live with integrity and not by cunning, everyone knows. Nevertheless, one sees from experience in our

times that the princes who have accomplished great
deeds [*aver fatto gran cose*] are those who have thought
little about keeping faith and who have known how cunningly to manipulate men's minds; and in the end they
have surpassed those who laid their foundations upon
sincerity.

Who might be the prince of his own times who has accomplished great deeds by being unfaithful Machiavelli only
vaguely alludes to at the end of the chapter:

A certain prince of the present times, whom it is best
not to name, preaches nothing but peace and faith, and
to both one and the other he is extremely hostile. If he
had observed both peace and faith, he would have had
either his reputation or his state taken away from him
many times over.

In chapter XXI, however, Machiavelli reveals that a fine
example of a prince who has accomplished great—in fact,
truly extraordinary—deeds is Ferdinand of Aragon:

Nothing makes a prince more esteemed than *great undertakings* [*grandi imprese*] and showing himself to be
extraordinary. In our own times we have Ferdinand of
Aragon, the present King of Spain. . . . If you consider
his deeds you will find them all *very grand*, and some
even extraordinary [*tutte grandissime e qualcuna estraordi-
naria*], . . . Besides this, in order to be able to undertake
great[er] enterprises [*maggiori imprese*], he had recourse
to a pious cruelty, always employing religion for his own

purposes, chasing the Marranos out of his kingdom and seizing their property. . . . And thus he has always accomplished and organized *great deeds* [*ha fatte e ordite cose grandi*], that have always kept the minds of his subjects surprised, amazed, and occupied with their outcome. One action of his would spring from another in such a way that, between one and the other, he would never give men enough time to be able to work calmly against him [italics mine].

Great and even extraordinary as they are, Ferdinand of Aragon's deeds do pale in comparison with those of ancient founders of states and redeemers of peoples like Moses, Cyrus, and Theseus, who created new and good political orders. "Nothing," asserts Machiavelli, "brings so much honor to a man newly risen up than the new laws and new institutions discovered by him. When these are well founded and have greatness in them [*abbino in loro grandezza*], they make a man revered and admirable." They are the only men whom Machiavelli calls "rare and marvelous"; the only ones whom Machiavelli explicitly and forcefully points as the examples to be followed. "This [the liberation of Italy from the barbarians] will not be very difficult if you keep before your eyes the deeds and the lives of those named above," and a few lines later, "Here circumstances are very favourable, and where circumstances are favourable there cannot be great difficulty, provided that you imitate the institutions of those men I have proposed as your targets."

Additional support for the view that the "Exhortation" concentrates *The Prince*'s main message comes from the letter to Francesco Vettori of December 10, 1513, in which

Machiavelli announces that he has composed a little essay "Of Principalities." Machiavelli's words are: "I have composed a short study *De Principatibus*. . . . I am continually fattening and currying it [*lo ingrasso e ripulisco*]."[2] "I have composed" means that by December 1513 the essay was, for the most part, completed. "I am continually fattening and currying it" means that at that time he was polishing and adding here and there. Machiavelli's words do not exclude that he added the "Exhortation" later. However, they indicate that he believed that his essay already contained all he wanted to say and was almost ready to be presented.

This interpretation is, however, open to a number of powerful objections that must be seriously considered. The first is that according to highly respected scholars, Machiavelli composed the "Exhortation" after December 1513, when we know that he had completed at least the main corpus of *The Prince*. Hans Baron, for instance, indicates as the most probable date January to March 1515; Sergio Bertelli suggests 1516; Mario Martelli claims that Machiavelli composed the last chapter much later than the other parts of his work, in 1518, to provide ideological and political support for Lorenzo de' Medici the Duke of Urbino's project to establish an absolute principality in central Italy.[3] Machiavelli, it has been claimed, saw in that young and ambitious man who had concentrated in his own hands an enormous power a possible redeemer of Italy and hastened to compose the "Exhortation" that was later appended to the rest of the manuscript. If we accept the view that Machiavelli composed the "Exhortation" in 1515 or in 1516, or later, it is utterly wrong to claim, as I do, that

Machiavelli composed *The Prince* to give life to a redeemer and a founder.

Even if these views are sustained by solid textual and historical considerations, I believe that I can claim that Machiavelli composed the "Exhortation," or at least a substantial part of it, along with the rest of *The Prince*, as its own necessary completion and conclusion, not as a later appendage.[4] The "Exhortation," to begin with, opens with an explicit reference to the considerations that he has discussed in the previous twenty-five chapters ("therefore, considering all the matters discussed above"), and it is conceptually connected with chapter VI, as I have shown. To make his case that circumstances are favorable for a new prince to introduce new political orders and liberate Italy from the barbarians, Machiavelli then refers to the position of preeminence reached by the House of the Medici as of March 1513: "Nor is there anyone in sight, at present, in whom she [Italy] can have more hope than in Your Illustrious House, which, with its fortune and virtue, favored by God and by the Church, of which it is now prince, could place itself at the head of this redemption."

The words we must focus our attention on are "of which it is *now* prince" ("della quale ora è principe"). The adverb *ora* in Italian refers to events that are very close in time. It is highly unlikely that a writer like Machiavelli would have used that adverb to denote an event that had occurred two or three or even five years before.[5] This suggests that he probably composed the "Exhortation" a few months after Giovanni de' Medici's elevation to the throne of Saint Peter in March 1513. The scholars who maintain

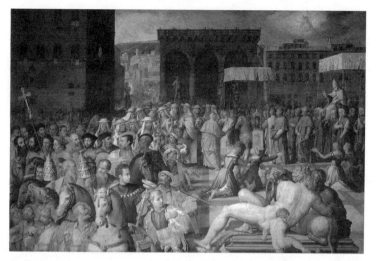

Figure 6. Giorgio Vasari and assistants, *Pope Leo X's Procession through Florence*. Sala di Leone X, Palazzo Vecchio, Florence, Italy. Photo: Scala / Art Resource, NY.

that Machiavelli composed the "Exhortation" having in mind an actual political occasion for the liberation of Italy are right, but such an occasion, in his view, materialized in 1513, when the head of the Medici family, Giovanni, was at the same time the de facto ruler of Florence and the prince of Christendom.

Additional textual evidence is to be found in that passage of the "Exhortation" where Machiavelli writes: "As a consequence, during so much time and so many wars waged during the past twenty years, whenever there has been an army made up completely of Italians, it has always made a poor showing. As a proof of this is Taro; then Alexandria, Capua, Genoa, Vailà, and Mestre." For Machiavelli, the total ineptitude of the Italian armies, due to their captains'

Figure 7. Francesco Granacci, *Entrance of Charles VIII in Florence.*
Uffizi, Florence, Italy. Photo: Scala / Art Resource, NY.

incompetence and lack of military valor, appeared in all its
gravity in 1494, when the King of France, Charles VIII,
invaded the peninsula. The phrase "during the past twenty
years" seems therefore to bring us closer to the end of 1513
than to 1515 or 1518.

For the purpose of identifying *The Prince*'s main subject
matter and message, it is very important to clarify that Machiavelli discusses the redemption of people and the foundations of new political orders also in other works, using a
language similar to that of the "Exhortation." In the preface
to book II of the *Discourses on Livy*, Machiavelli writes:

> I will be spirited in saying manifestly that which I may
> understand of the former and of the latter times [the
> times on the ancient Romans and modern times], so
> that the spirits of youths who may read these writings of

mine can flee the latter and prepare themselves to imitate the former at whatever time fortune may give them
the opportunity [*occasione*] for it. For it is the duty of a
good man to teach others the good that you could not
work because of the malignity of the times and of fortune, so that when many are capable of it, someone of
them more loved by heaven [*più amato dal cielo*] may be
able to work it.

In the *Discourse on Remodeling the State of Florence*, he
writes an eloquent invocation to a reformer of the political
orders of Florence:

> No man is so much exalted by any act of his as are those
> men who have with laws and with institutions remod-
> eled republics and kingdoms; these are, after those who
> have been gods, the first to be praised. And because there
> have been few who have had opportunity to do it, and
> very few those who have understood how to do it, small
> is the number who have done it. And so much has this
> glory been esteemed by men seeking for nothing other
> than glory that when unable to form a republic in real-
> ity, they have done it in writing, as Aristotle, Plato, and
> many others, who have wished to show the world that if
> they have not founded a free government, as did Solon
> and Lycurgus, they have failed not through their igno-
> rance but through their impotence for putting it into
> practice.[6]

The *Art of War* (1521) ends with the evocation of new
political leaders capable of offering the kind of political

advice that would help to resuscitate Italy from its present condition of corruption and servitude.[7] In the *Florentine Histories*, he expresses his hope that in Florence,

> by the good fortune of a city there rises in it a wise, good and powerful citizen by whom laws are ordered by which these humors of the nobles and the men of the people are quieted or restrained so that they cannot do evil, then the city can be called free and the state be judged stable and firm: for a city based on good laws and good orders has no necessity, as have others, for the virtue of a single man to maintain it.[8]

Machiavelli, it must be stressed, believed in the power of poetry and myths to inspire political redeemers. In the *Florentine Histories*, he writes about the failed conspiracy of Stefano Porcari in Rome:

> Living at that time was a Messer Stefano Porcari [early 1400–1453], a Roman citizen, noble by blood and by learning, but much more so by the excellence of his spirit. This man desired, according to the custom of men who relish glory, to do or at least to try something worthy of memory; and he judged he could do nothing else than try to see if he could take his fatherland from the hands of prelates and restore it to its ancient way of life, hoping by this, should he succeed, to be called the new founder and second father of that city.[9]

Machiavelli then writes, and this is the phrase I want to focus on, "The dissolute manners of the priesthood, and the discontent of the Roman barons and people, encouraged him to look for a happy termination of his enterprise," but he derived his greatest confidence from those verses of Petrarch in the canzone that begins, "Spirto gentil che quelle membra reggi," where he says:

Sopra il monte Tarpeio, canzon, vedrai
Un cavalier che Italia tutta onora,
Pensoso più d'altrui che di se stesso.

Atop Mount Tarpeio, Oh ! canzone, you will see
A knight whom all Italy honors
More thoughtful of others than of himself

These are, for me, the key words:

> Messer Stefano knew that many times poets are filled with divine and prophetic spirit; so he judged that in any mode the thing Petrarch had prophesied in that canzone must come, and that it was he who ought to be the executor of so glorious an undertaking, since it appeared to him that he was superior to every Roman in eloquence, learning, grace, and friends.[10]

Machiavelli, I want to stress, ends *The Prince* with Petrarch's verses in the hope that his poetry will inspire a new redeemer:

Virtue will seize arms
Against furor, and the battle will be brief:

For ancient valour
Is not yet dead in Italian hearts

Machiavelli cherished the hope, or, better, the illusion, of the coming of a political redeemer until the last days of his life, when he dedicated his remaining energies to the desperate effort of preventing Italy's fall under the domination of Charles V. On March 15, 1526, he wrote Guicciardini, who was committed, with much greater political and military responsibilities, to the same task, a dramatic letter that reveals that he was hoping that Giovanni de' Medici (Giovanni dalla Bande Nere) could be the redeemer of Italy:

> I am going to tell you one thing that you will think absurd; I shall put forward a plan that you will consider either rash or ridiculous: nevertheless, these times of our demand bold, extraordinary, and unusual decisions. You know—and anyone who knows how to reason about this world knows it, too—that the people are fickle and foolish; nevertheless, as fickle and foolish as they are, what ought to be done is frequently what they say to do. A few days ago it was being said throughout Florence that Giovanni de' Medici was raising a company of mercenaries in order to fight wherever he saw the best opportunity. The rumor alerted me to consider whether the people might not be saying what in fact ought to be done. I believe everyone is agreed that among Italians there is no leader whom the soldiers more willingly follow or whom the Spaniards fear more or respect more

than Signor Giovanni. Everyone also agrees that he is brave and impetuous, has great ideas, and is a taker of bold decisions. Therefore we could get him to raise this mercenary company, secretly enlarging his forces, helping him to raise a banner and putting under his command as much infantry and cavalry as possible.[11]

A leader capable of attempting great things, willing to raise a banner and put together a fine army composed of captains and soldiers who love and wholeheartedly follow him—the same ideas of the "Exhortation" resurface once again. In *The Prince*, he appealed to the prophetic force of a poet; in this letter, he wants to believe in the people's prophetic power. Not without cause, he writes in the *Discourses*, "may the voice of a people be likened to that of God: for one sees a universal opinion produce marvelous effects in its forecast, so that it appears to foresee its ills and its goods by a hidden virtue."[12]

A few months later, upon the news that tumults against the Spaniards had burst out in Milan, he launches yet again the idea of the "Exhortation" that there is another great occasion to liberate Italy, one not to be missed: "You are aware of how many opportunities have been lost: do not lose this one or, putting yourself in the hands of Fortune and Time, trust in having it again, because Time does not always bring identical circumstances and Fortune is not always the same." Many years had elapsed since he had written the "Exhortation," many events had occurred in Italy and in his life, and he was now an old man, at the end of his life, but the determination to liberate his country from the barbarians is still in his mind and his will: "Free Italy from long-lasting anxiety: eradicate those savage brutes, which have nothing human about them save their faces and voices." That a man whose dominant passion for all his life has been love of country, and whose dominant concern has been the redemption of Italy has composed a work to design and invoke a redeeming prince, not just a prince like all the others, seems to me to be, on the basis of the texts that I have examined, a rather reasonable interpretation.

Of True Greatness

To assert that *The Prince*'s most important political message is about the redemption of Italy must sound rather implausible for a text that opens with a dedicatory letter to Lorenzo di Piero di Lorenzo de' Medici and ends with an "Exhortation" that explicitly indicates the house of the Medici as the historical agent of Italy's liberation and unification. This objection is less damaging to my interpretation than it might appear to be, for two reasons. The first is that Machiavelli himself suggests that the text of *The Prince* and the dedicatory letter are separate.[13] A careful reading of his words is revealing:

> And because Dante says that to have understood without retaining does not make knowledge, I *have noted* what capital I have made from their conversation [the conversation with the ancient men] and *have composed* [*e composto*] a little work *De Principatibus* [On Principalities], where I delve as deeply as I can into reflections on this subject, debating what a principality is, of what kinds they are, how they are acquired, how they are maintained, why they are lost. And if you have ever been pleased by

any of my whimsies, this one should not displease you: and to a prince, and especially to a new prince, it should be welcome. So *I am addressing* [*però io lo indirizzo*] it to his Magnificence, Giuliano [italics mine].

Machiavelli is telling us that in *The Prince*, he has distilled the knowledge of principalities that he has attained through his reflections on ancient histories and modern events, and afterward he considered dedicating it to Giuliano. We can still believe that Machiavelli composed the *De Principatibus* having in mind, since the very beginning, to please the Medici, but the letter suggests a different sequence between the stages of reflection, composition, and dedication.[14]

The second reason is that nowhere in the text of *The Prince* does Machiavelli explicitly or implicitly refer to the Medici.[15] He mentions the "Illustrious House" of the Medici four times in the "Exhortation," to urge them to imitate the great founders and redeemers. In this respect, Machiavelli's text is quite different from other advice books for princes, as the titles of a number of them make clear. Francesco Petrarca, *Ad Magnificum Franciscum de Carraria Padue dominum qualis esse debeat qui rempublicam regit*, for instance, is a long epistle with references to private conversations with Francesco de Carrara and to specific episodes of his life. After having explained at length that a prince is safer when he is loved and not when he is feared by his subjects, Petrarch frames his advice in terms of a personal recommendation:

Indeed, from the discussion of this topic nothing but immense and honourable pleasure ought to come to you since you are so beloved by your subjects that you seem to them to be not a lord over citizens but the "father of your country." . . . There is no one among your citizens (that is among those who really seek the peace and the well-being of Padua) who looks upon you otherwise, who thinks of you as anything other than a father. But you have to continue to strive so that you merit this dignity; it endures forever because of your noble efforts.[16]

Among classical Ciceronian precepts on justice, mercy, and liberality, Petrarch does not miss the opportunity to insert a piece of advice that can hardly be taken as a general prescription on rulership:

I have never known anyone—and I am not speaking here of princes but of every sort of men—except perhaps your own dear father, who likes to ride on horseback, as you do, into every part of his country for such long stretches of time. I am not criticizing this habit of yours since your first duty and care is clearly the good government of Padua, and the presence of a good prince is always pleasing to faithful citizens but you ought to take care that what you do so eagerly you also do safely. Hence you should remove all danger and difficulties from this horseback-riding and turn it into an agreeable and pleasant recreation.[17]

Giovanni Pontano in his *De Principe* (1468) directs all his counsels directly to Alphonsus Duke of Calabria, and when he points to examples, he explicitly mentions the Duke's father, Ferdinand, or his grandfather, Alphonsus.[18]

When he stresses that a prince must be humane, Pontano begins his argument with a personal reference: "even if you excel in this virtue," it is necessary that you are loved not only by your relatives but also by everyone.[19] And when he explains that a prince must reward virtue, Pontano writes: "Since you are the successor of the great and wealthy kingdom of Naples, I warmly exhort you to learn to follow since your childhood the footsteps of your father and of your grandfather, and to get used to looking for the company of the most esteemed and virtuous men."[20] Last, in the conclusion, Pontano reassures the young duke that his intention was not to teach him but to offer him the opportunity to recognize himself and his most praised deeds.[21]

Agostino Nifo, who follows Machiavelli's impersonal style of writing on principalities and princes, promptly states in the title itself that his book is written for the Emperor Charles V: *De regnandi peritia ad Carolum V Imper. Caesarem Semper Augustus* (Naples, 1523). Bartholomeus Sacchi (Il Platina) (1523) dedicated his *De Principe* to the heir of the Gonzaga dukedom and the reigning prince in Mantua, Luigi Gonzaga. To persuade the duke to respect Christian religion with the utmost devotion, Platina makes first a general point on the political usefulness of religion, and then extols the duke's ancestors for their devotion in defense of the Christian faith against corrupt prelates.[22] Also the injunction to cultivate love of country is specifically addressed.[23] Having asserted the conventional humanist principle that only virtue confers true nobility, Platina rapidly proceeds to recognize the whole Gonzaga lineage as a shining example of generosity and the ability to choose friends who encourage them to pursue virtue and glory.[24]

This does not mean that Machiavelli was not thinking about the Medici while he was writing his pages. It
just means that Machiavelli's chief motivation to compose
his essay was not to please the Medici and to get a job
from them. Had this been the case, he would have written
a quite different text, full of praise for the Medici and for
their glorious history, replete with the kind of counsel that
men like Giuliano, Giulio, Lorenzo, or Leo X liked to hear.
Machiavelli knew better than anyone else that the most
important rule of successful flattery is to say what pleases
the person from which one expects to obtain favors. In *The
Prince*, he does exactly the opposite. Instead of repeating
the well-established principles that had allowed the Medici
to gain control over the city, Machiavelli gives them advice
that they were not in the least able to appreciate and that
would surely have irritated them, had they read his work.
He was not a follower of the Medici; he wanted the Medici
to follow him.

An evident criticism of the Medici's art of the state is
Machiavelli's harsh assessment of their policy of patronage
and favors: "Friendships that are acquired with money, and
not through greatness and nobility of character, are paid
for but not secured, and prove unreliable just when they are
needed."[25] By friendship acquired with money, Machiavelli
means the practice of gaining support and loyalty through
private favors of various sorts. In the *Discorsi*, he calls this
private, as opposed to public, modes of attaining reputation:

> The public modes are when individual one acquires
> reputation by counseling well and acting well for the
> common benefit. The way to such honors ought to be

opened to every citizen, and rewards proposed for their good counsels and good works, so that they may obtain honors and be satisfied: and when such reputation is obtained through these pure and simple ways, it will never be dangerous: but when it is obtained through a private way (which is the other method mentioned) it is most dangerous and wholly harmful. The private ways are by doing good to this and that private individual by lending them money, marrying their daughters, defending them in front of Magistrates, and doing them similar private favors, which make men partisans, and give encouragement to whoever is thus favored to be able to corrupt the public and break the laws.[26]

These practices, Machiavelli warns, seem "pious"—in fact, they conceal the "beginning of tyranny." Because they appear to be inspired by the desire to benefit citizens, it is extremely difficult to successfully fight them. In the *Florentine Histories*, Machiavelli cites on this subject the words of the most wise Niccolò da Uzano (1359–1431) on Cosimo de' Medici the Elder:

> Those actions of Cosimo which lead us to suspect him are, that he lends money indiscriminately, and not to private persons only, but to the public; and not to Florentines only, but to the *condottieri*, the soldiers of fortune. Besides, he assists any citizen who requires magisterial aid; and, by the universal interest he possesses in the city, raises first one friend and then another to higher grades of honor. Therefore, to adduce our reasons for expelling him, would be to say that he is kind, generous, liberal,

and beloved by all. Now tell me, what law is there which
forbids, disapproves, or condemns men for being pious,
liberal, and benevolent? And though they are all modes
adopted by those who aim at sovereignty, they are not
believed to be such, nor have we sufficient power to
make them to be so esteemed.[27]

Machiavelli's political conclusion is the same as in the *Discourses*: "private modes" are incompatible with the common
good and therefore destroy republican life.

Whereas in the *Discourses on Livy* and in the *Florentine
Histories* Machiavelli denounces the practice of attaining
reputation through money and favors, in which the Medici
excelled, as a way to establish a veiled tyranny within republican institutions, in *The Prince* he contrasts it with the
friendships that a prince gains through the greatness and
nobility of his spirit. He claims that friendships attained
through money are not a secure foundation for his power
because "One can generally say this about men: they are
ungrateful, fickle, simulators and deceivers, avoiders of danger and greedy for gain. While you work for their benefit
they are completely yours, offering you their blood, their
property, their lives, and their sons, as I said above, when
the need to do so is far away. But when it draws nearer
to you, they turn away." The contrast between friendships
acquired with money and friendships acquired through
greatness and nobility of character is yet further evidence
that Machiavelli intended to teach a lesson about grand
politics, not to offer counsel on how to replicate in Florence
a petty regime like the ones that the Medici had established since the time of Cosimo the Elder. He rejects the

Medicean policy of favors because he has in mind another kind of political action, that of founders and redeemers. It is this kind of political action that requires true greatness and nobility of spirit.

What does Machiavelli actually mean by greatness and nobility of spirit? He recognizes greatness of spirit in Cosimo the Elder when he was regretting his own inability to expand the Florentine dominion. He also acknowledges the greatness of spirit of Lorenzo the Magnificent when he had the courage to sail for Naples and meet the king who was at the time one of the most determined and dangerous enemies of Florence.[28] Though marred by a number of serious vices, Machiavelli also granted greatness of spirit to Agathocles of Syracuse.[29]

In addition to chapter XVII of *The Prince*, Machiavelli speaks of greatness of soul and nobility together only in the chapter of the *Discourses* where he discusses the transition from tyranny to aristocracy in the cycle of governments: "These conspiracies against the prince were not made by weak and timid men, but by those who because of their generosity, greatness of spirit, riches, and nobility above the others, could not endure the dishonest life of that prince."[30] The most eloquent examples of greatness and nobility of spirit are however, as I have already stressed, those marvelous and rare men who have founded new and good political orders. Moses distinguished himself for his "virtue"; Cyrus for his "greatness of spirit"; Theseus for his "excellence"; Romulus was "virtuous and prudent." Their political deeds reflect the greatness and nobility of their spirits.

In the hierarchy of excellence that he sets in the *Discourses on Livy*, Machiavelli ranks the great founders second only

to the founders of religions. In a later work he composed
around 1520, he refers to them as almost divine figures.[31]
Because of their greatness and nobility of spirit, founders
generate in their people the obedience, love, and devotion
that is necessary to accomplish great political deeds: "Nor
can I express with what love he will be received in all those
territories that have suffered through these foreign floods;
with what thirst for revenge, with what stubborn loyalty,
with what devotion, with what tears! What doors will be
closed to him? What people will deny him their obedience?
What envy could oppose him? What Italian could deny
him homage?" A politics of favors through money could
never produce anything like that. That is what makes it severely inadequate. Machiavelli wrote *The Prince* for a new
Moses, not for another Cosimo the Elder.

The central role that the concept of greatness assumes
in *The Prince* emerges also in one of the most controversial
sections of the whole work—namely, chapter IX, "Of Civil
Principality." Some scholars argue that here Machiavelli
was urging the Medici to abandon their traditional practice
of ruling behind the scenes through magistrates they were
able to control and to institute an absolute principality in
which they came to the forefront and openly governed the
city with no limitations to their power. Others have maintained that Machiavelli was in fact dissuading them, and
any other prince, from making such a move because of the
evident dangers it presents.[32]

Understandably, the whole issue was hotly debated,
in Florence and in Rome, in the early years of the new
Medicean regime (1512–18). The different positions held
by the most prominent friends of the House of the Medici

can be divided in two main camps. The first group maintained that the fresh memory of the popular republic of
1494–1512 was a formidable obstacle to the consolidation
of the new regime. Under that regime, they stressed, the
people of Florence had a liberty that they had never en-
joyed, and the large majority of them were still hoping to
retrieve it. From this, they concluded that the Medici had
no hope of gaining the people's loyalty through the traditional practice of ruling behind the scenes, through favors
and patronage. What they needed to do, therefore, was to
openly become princes of Florence, govern with the support of the noble families, and rely on military force to keep
the nostalgic friends of the popular regime quiet.[33]

Other counselors eloquently argued that the Medici
ought instead to continue the tradition of "civil principality" that Cosimo the Elder had so successfully initiated
and brought to unsurpassed perfection.[34] That policy, they
stressed, had permitted Cosimo and Lorenzo to overcome
hurdles much greater that the present ones, and there was
therefore no need to embark on risky political adventures.
Instead, the key preoccupation of the new regime should
have been to control the main institutions of Florentine
government, select a core group of advisors, and continue
to govern the city in the good old manner.

Machiavelli, who was surely aware of this discussion,[35]
enters in the debate by setting first his own definition of
the civil principality:

> But let us come to the second instance, when a private
> citizen becomes prince of his native city not through
> wickedness or any other intolerable violence, but with

the favor of his fellow citizens. This can be called a civil principality, the acquisition of which neither depends completely upon virtue nor upon fortune, but instead upon a fortunate astuteness.[36]

He then proceeds to dismantle all the premises of the arguments in favor of the transition from a civil to an open principality, beginning with the view that the memory of the past popular government was an almost invincible enemy of the Medici regime. The truth of the matter, he writes, is that "men are much more taken by present concerns than by those of the past, and when they discover benefit in present things, they enjoy it and seek no more. In fact, they will seize every measure to defend the new prince so long as he is not neglectful of his duties."[37] With his typical briskness, he also puts to rest the view that the most dangerous enemies of the Medici were the people of Florence in general, and the supporters of the past regime in particular. The true danger, he claims, does not come from those who were content with the popular government, but from the aristocrats who were dissatisfied with it. It will be very difficult for the new prince to turn them into loyal friends, even if they have helped him to attain power.[38] A new prince must therefore always regard the aristocrats as a serious threat to the state because they have the means and the audacity to openly attack him, if they are dissatisfied.

Machiavelli's conclusion is that between a civil principality founded on the people's support and a civil principality founded on the nobles' support, the first type is much safer than the second. On the methods that a prince should use to gain and maintain the people's support, Machiavelli is rather vague: "a prince can gain their favor in various ways, but because they vary according to the situation, no fixed rules can be given for them, and therefore I shall not discuss them." The conclusion of chapter IX is also ambivalent:

> Principalities of that type [civil principalities] are usually endangered when they are about to change from a civil government into an absolute form of government. For these princes rule either by themselves or by means of public magistrates. In the latter case, their status is weaker and more dangerous, since they depend entirely upon the will of those citizens who are appointed as magistrates. These men can very easily (especially in adverse times) seize the state, either by abandoning him or by opposing him. And in such periods of danger the prince has no time for seizing absolute authority, since the citizens and subjects who are used to receiving their orders from the magistrates are not willing to obey his orders in these crises.

And this experiment, Machiavelli warns in a rather dramatic tone, "is all the more dangerous since it can be tried but once."[39]

To write that a particular course of action is exceedingly dangerous is a dissuasion, not an encouragement. Machiavelli, however, also rejects the idea of just carrying on the old policy of governing indirectly by controlling through the friends of the house the committees of Florentine government. The civil principality is—like the policy of friendship acquired by a price—inadequate to sustain the

initiative of a redeemer. What then is Machiavelli's advice?
It is, once again, the politics of greatness: when "the prince
who builds his foundations on the people is a man able
to command and of spirit, is not bewildered by adversities,
does not fail to make other preparations, and is a leader
who keeps up the spirits of the populace through his courage and his institutions, he will never find himself deceived
by the common people, and he will discover that he has
laid down his foundations well."[40] Only this kind of politics
would have ensured security and glory to a new prince, had
he decided to listen to Machiavelli.

THE AUTHOR OF *THE PRINCE*

If we want to better illuminate the meaning of *The Prince*, we
must now abandon for a while the text and concentrate our
attention on the author to try to identify his beliefs and passions. In the case of Machiavelli, this work is rather simple,
since we have all the evidence we could want that his overwhelming passion was his love of country. As is well known,
he wrote in one of his last letters, on April 16, 1527, "I love
my *patria* [fatherland] more than my own soul." Six years
before, when he was in Carpi to discharge a quite inglori-
ous mission on behalf of the Wool Guild of Florence, Machiavelli had no hesitation to flatly explain to Guicciardini,
at the time governor of the papal states of Modena and
Reggio, that he took very seriously his duty, even if it was
quite humbling for a man like him: "And because never did
I disappoint that republic whenever I was able to help her
out—if not with deeds, then with words; if not with words,
then with signs—I have no intention of disappointing her

now."[41] In Machiavelli's case, these were not just mere proc-
lamations. His life proves that love of country was one of
his deepest and lasting passions. He proudly proclaimed
that his poverty was the evidence that when he was the Segretario, from 1498 to 1512 , he served his fatherland with
impeccable devotion, faith, and honesty.[42] Even if Florence
had been ungrateful and unjust to him, he never considered
leaving it, not even when he was offered an excellent opportunity, in 1521, to move to Ragusa to be again at the service
of the former Gonfalonier of the Republic, Pier Soderini.[43]
He chose to stay even if all that his fatherland was offering
him were really meager honors and poor jobs.[44] Who else
could have written a text like the "Exhortation," if not a
man who so sincerely loved his fatherland?

When Niccolò set down in his country house in
Sant'Andrea in Percussina in the summer of 1513 to reflect on principalities and princes, he was a deeply wounded
man. The Medicean regime that had been established in
Florence in September 1512 and had removed him from
his post as Segretario of the Second Chancery of the Republic and of the Ten in November 1512 took away from
him not only his job and his social status but also the most
precious commodity in his life—the possibility to dedicate
himself to political action. Detached from real political action, Niccolò no longer knew who he was. All he knew was
that he was no longer the Segretario—he was the "former
secretary" ("quondam segretario"), as he signed a letter to
Vettori on April 9, 1513.

His letters from March through December 1513 reveal a man deeply afflicted, but still hoping to be able to
resurrect and fight back against the malignity of men and

Figure 8. Machiavelli's farmhouse in Sant'Andrea in Percussina, where he composed *The Prince*. Courtesy Vignaccia76, Wikimedia Commons.

fortune. On June 26, for instance, he wrote to his nephew Giovanni Vernacci:

> My very dear Giovanni, I have received several letters from you, most recently one from last April in which, among other things, you complain that you have not received any letter from me. My answer is that since your departure I have had so much trouble that it is no wonder I have not written to you. In fact, if anything, it is a miracle that I am alive, because my post was taken from me and I was about to lose my life, which God and my innocence have preserved for me. I have had to endure all sorts of other evils, both prison and other kinds. But,

Figure 9. Another view of Machiavelli's farmhouse in Sant'Andrea
in Percussina. Courtesy Don MacDonald.

by the grace of God, I am well and I manage to live as I
can—and so I shall strive to do until the heavens show
themselves to be more kind.[45]

On August 4, he confessed that "physically I feel well, but
ill in every other respect. And no hope remains for me but
that God may help me, and, until now, He has not in fact
abandoned me."[46]

The correspondence of the summer of 1514 shows Niccolò in a completely different spirit. On June 10, 1514, he
wrote to Francesco Vettori:

So I am going to stay just as I am amid my bedbugs, unable to find any man who recalls my service or believes

I might be good for anything. But I cannot possibly go on like this for long, because I am rotting away and I can see that if God does not show a more favorable face to me, one day I shall be forced to leave home and to place myself as tutor or secretary to a governor, if I cannot do otherwise, or to stick myself in some deserted spot to teach reading to children and leave my family here to count me dead; they will do much better without me because I am causing them expenses, since I am used to spending and I cannot do without spending.[47]

Even more important, for my argument, is the letter of August 3, 1514, in which Machiavelli informed Vettori that in Sant'Andrea in Percussina he had met a woman "so gracious, so refined, so noble—both in nature and in manners—that never could either my praise or my love for her be as much as she deserves." Faithful to his principle that human beings must follow their nature, if they want to taste some measure of happiness, Machiavelli let himself pursue this passion. He believed, at least for a while, that love could cure his torment. "I have laid aside all memory of my sorrows," he wrote. Even the grand deeds of great men of antiquity no longer interested him: "I have renounced then, thoughts about matters great and grave. No longer do I delight in reading about the deeds of the ancients or in discussing those of the moderns: everything has been transformed into tender thoughts, for which I thank Venus and all Cyprus."[48]

This is a remarkable confession. Machiavelli is telling us that he has abandoned ("lasciato") his thoughts about matters grave and grand, and that reading and thinking and writing about the deeds of the ancients, *no longer* delights him as it used to ("non mi diletta più"). It is exactly the opposite spirit that he described in the letter of December 10, 1513, when thinking, reading and writing about grand deeds, had *then* the power of liberating him from his fears ("for four hours I feel no boredom, forget all troubles, fear not poverty, am not anguished by death: I simply give myself over to them completely").

As time went by, Machiavelli's mood was even more melancholic and depressed. On January 31, 1515, he confessed to Vettori that he was in love again, but he also revealed that Donato Del Corno and his lover were "the sole havens and refuges for [his] skiff—bereft of rudder and sail because of the unending tempest."[49] On August 18, 1515, he described to Giovanni Vernacci his personal condition in the most disconsolate manner: "If I have not written to you earlier, I do not want you to blame either me or anyone else, but only the times; they have been—and still are—of such a sort that they have made me forget even myself."[50]

The fall brought no consolation to Niccolò: "I have written to you twice during the last four months, and I am sorry that you have not received them, because it occurs to me that you will think I do not write because I have forgotten all about you. That is not true at all: Fortune has left me nothing but my family and my friends."[51] On February 15, 1516, Machiavelli spoke of himself as a man "useless" to himself, to his family, and to his friends. All he was left with was his "good health" and that of his family: "I bide my time so that I may be ready to seize good fortune should she come; should she not come, I am ready to be patient."[52] In

June 1517, Machiavelli's condition was even worse: "Since the adversities that I have suffered, and still I am suffering, have reduced me to living on my farm, I sometimes go for a month at a time without thinking about myself," he wrote to Vernacci.[53] The letters of January 5 and January 25, 1518, reveal once again a man who feels "harshly beaten by malignant luck" and utterly disheartened.[54]

This is surely not conclusive evidence, but I cannot imagine a person in such a condition being capable of writing a text full of strength, determination, and hope such as the "Exhortation." I am neither attempting to produce a psychological study nor am I suggesting some kind of causal connection between Machiavelli's existential condition and the text. More modestly, I claim that the study of Machiavelli's life—in particular, the interpretation of his passions and beliefs—helps us to understand the meaning of *The Prince* and to better identify the date of composition of the "Exhortation."[55]

The ideal of the redeemer capable of uniting the forces of Italy and liberating it from the domination of foreign powers was probably the original inspiration that encouraged Machiavelli to write his essay. As early as August 10, 1513, he had clearly expressed his view that Italy's miserable condition was the consequence of the lack of a true unity and of a political and military leader. His argument, and even his choice of words, evoke the "Exhortation" and chapter XXV on fortune: "As for the rest of the Italians uniting, you make me laugh: first there will never be any union in Italy that will do any good; even if all leaders were united, that would be inadequate because the armies here are not worth a red cent—except for the Spaniards', and because there are so few of them, it is insufficient. Second the tails are cut off from the heads."[56]

For a man like Machiavelli, in the condition in which he found himself after November 1512, the only way he saw to be able to live the kind of life he wanted to live, and to be again the man he used to be, was to compose a treatise that would convince everyone that he was the most qualified person to give solid advice on grand and grave political matters, even if he was only the "former" Segretario: "And through this study of mine, were it to be read, it would be evident that during the fifteen years I have been studying the art of the state I have neither slept nor fooled around, and anybody ought to be happy to utilize someone who has had so much experience at the expenses of others."[57]

It was Vettori who openly encouraged him to think again about political matters and told him that even if he was no longer the Segretario, he surely had not lost the remarkable talent that everyone in Florence admired.[58] Reluctantly, Machiavelli accepted Vettori's prompt and made an effort to fight melancholia and depression by writing on the subjects he loved in the hope that the Medici would recognize his competence and call him back to serve in office. But it was above all for himself that he composed the little essay: to be able to believe that he was still himself and that he deserved to stay in the company of the greatest men: "I enter the ancient courts of ancient men, where, received by them lovingly, I feed on the food that alone is mine. There I am not ashamed to speak with them and to ask them the reason for their actions; and they in their humanity reply to me." They were glad to talk to him because they recognized his competence on the issues of redemption and foundation and because they admired him for his love of country and of glory—the same passions that had inspired them to accomplish their deeds. For Niccolò, their friendship truly meant a lot. It was the greatest motivation to write *The Prince*.

CHAPTER TWO

A Realist with Imagination

ARMIES, IMAGINATION, AND RELIGION

At this stage of my argument, I must address another serious objection to the view that *The Prince*'s fundamental message is about political emancipation and redemption—namely, Machiavelli's much celebrated (or blamed) realism. The image of the founder and redeemer that he shapes is clearly a work of imagination, even if he was exhorting real human beings like the Medici to assume that role and suggested that someone like the Duke Valentino had some of the necessary qualities of a new prince. By imagination, I mean here the intellectual effort to conceive a political and moral reality that is radically different from the existing one and yet, unlike castles in the air, represents and reflects deep and historically serious aspirations and has therefore the power to move people to action and to become, at least in part, real. But Machiavelli himself, as has been endlessly noted over the centuries, has flatly told us that his *Prince* was a work based on the study of the "effectual truth of the matter" (*la realtà effettuale della cosa*), not a work of political imagination. Yet in all his works, and in *The Prince* above all, Machiavelli did not give up political imagination at all. He surely was a realist, but a realist of a special sort—let's call him a realist with imagination. My purpose in this chapter is to clarify this claim.

Analytically trained readers may resist my assertion, protest that the concept of a realist with imagination is surely an oxymoron, and stress that Machiavelli must be either a realist or an imaginative theorist, to avoid the shameful charge of inconsistency. To defend my view, I begin by stressing that Machiavelli himself in a number of letters asserted as clearly as possible that the right way of living and thinking is to intelligently accommodate different and even contradictory aspects of human life, like passions and reason, gravity and lightness, civic integrity and playful transgression.[1] He also openly revealed his inclination to daydreaming and imagining political events.[2] In the gloomiest days of his life, we learn from a letter to Ludovico Alamanni of December 17, 1517, Machiavelli found consolation imagining, with some friends, a trip to Flanders that evoked utopian literature.[3] After all, we should not forget that Machiavelli has also been famous for a dream ("il sogno di Machiavelli") that it was said he described on his deathbed.[4]

The opinions of Machiavelli's friends also indicate that Niccolò was a rather special sort of political realist. Francesco Guicciardini, the true example of political realism, considered Machiavelli a political thinker too keen to generalize and to interpret political events through abstract models and examples taken from antiquity. With subtle irony, in a letter of May 1521, Guicciardini reproached Machiavelli for his inclination to discuss general forms of government such as monarchy, aristocracy, and republic. In his notes on the *Discourses on Livy*, he remarked that it was a mistake to always cite the example of the ancient Romans, as Machiavelli did so many times, because each situation is unique, and contingent. Political decisions should not therefore be taken by looking at abstract models but by using *discrezione* (discretion)—that is, a highly refined form of political prudence that is not based on general rules, that cannot be learned in books, and that very few men have by nature or are able to attain through a long practice.[5]

For Guicciardini, Machiavelli was also too keen to suggest highly unusual, perhaps effective, but surely risky courses of political action. In the midst of the dramatic political and military crisis of 1525–27 that led to the sack of Rome, for instance, Machiavelli proposed to Guicciardini and Pope Clement VII that the only way to save Italy and preserve the integrity of the papal state was to arm the people of Romagna and mobilize them against the invasion of imperial troops. To arm and organize the subjects of Romagna in a militia, Guicciardini replied, would be "one of the most useful and praiseworthy works that His Holiness could undertake," if only it were possible. Given the conditions of papal states in Romagna, it was, however, very dangerous. The people were torn by chronic political hostilities, and the Church had neither partisans nor friends there: those who wished to live well and peacefully disliked the Church because they wanted a government that would protect them; troublemakers and evil men disliked the Church because they saw disorder and war as a chance to settle accounts and see to their own interests.[6] Machiavelli's proposal was fascinating, but it did not pass the scrutiny of a genuine political realist. As Roberto Ridolfi, the biographer of Machiavelli and Guicciardini, has stressed, one should always read Machiavelli to find illuminations about the future, and Guicciardini to understand what was really going on in the political life of their times.[7]

What really distinguishes Machiavelli's realism from that of Guicciardini and many others like him was his persuasion that at times "rare and marvellous men" appear on the world's stage (perhaps sent by God) and do accomplish grand things like unifying scattered peoples, emancipating nations, and resurrecting political liberty. For him, men like Moses, Cyrus, Theseus, and Romulus were real, though special, and he believed that others like them might come. Guicciardini could not have even conceived the possibility of composing an exhortation like that of *The Prince*. Indeed, he tried to compose an exhortation, as a purely rhetorical exercise. He put on paper an imaginary oration to be presented to Leo X and Francis I, on occasion of their meeting in Bologna, in November 1515, to persuade them to launch a crusade to free Christ's sepulchre. Guicciardini's words echo Machiavelli's language of the "Exhortation," but the work remained unfinished.[8] Machiavelli, instead, after having explained, in the most realistic manner, what a new prince should do to preserve a principality, openly invoked a redeemer to liberate Italy from the barbarians. He stressed that such an extraordinary achievement would be possible, and indeed easy, because times were ripe for it. But he was imagining a grandiose event that existed only in his heart and in his mind.[9] No other political writer of his time, or of later centuries, combined the strictest adherence

to the rule that the knowledge of political reality comes
before political imagination, and at the same time inte-
grated the study of reality with the most powerful political imagination.

Machiavelli was also keen to create political myths from
the observation of political events. An example is his treatment of Caterina Sforza, the Duchess of Forlì, whom he
met in 1499 in his first important diplomatic mission. Fifteen years or so later, he wrote in the *Discourses*:

> Some Forlì conspirators killed Count Girolamo, their
> lord, and took his wife and his children, who were small.
> Since it appeared to them that they could not live se-
> curely if they did not become masters of the fortress,
> and the castellan was not willing to give it to them, Ma-
> donna Caterina (so the countess was called) promised
> the conspirators that if they let her enter it, she would
> deliver it to them and they might keep her children with
> them as hostages. Under this faith they let her enter it.
> As soon as she was inside, she reproved them from the
> walls for the death of her husband and threatened them
> with every kind of revenge. And to show that she did
> not care for her children, she showed them her geni-
> tal parts, saying that she still had the mode for making
> more of them.[10]

Eyewitness chroniclers have left us a very different account.
They wrote that Caterina was left out of the negotiations
with the conspirators by the castellan, who feared that Caterina, attached as she was to her sons, would have been too

Figure 10. Giorgio Vasari, *Portrait of Caterina Sforza*.
Palazzo Vecchio, Florence, Italy. Alinari / Art Resource, NY.

vulnerable to the conspirators' requests. Precisely because Machiavelli had met Caterina in person, he should have reported the historical truth rather than making up a legend. During his mission to Forlì, he had in fact seen with his own eyes Caterina neglecting affairs of state because she was "indisposed and in bad spirits over the great illness that befell Lodovico, her and Giovanni de' Medici's son." Yet he preferred to accept, and hand down to posterity, the account of Caterina smothering her own love for her offspring, knowing full well that it was a legend. With the help of classical sources, probably Tacitus and Plutarch, Machiavelli created a myth.[11] He wanted to offer a vivid example of true princely virtue, and to this effect he aptly transformed what he heard, and the historical record, into an inspiring narration.

An even more impressive example of Machiavelli's skill at mythologizing the characters he met during his diplomatic missions is his treatment of Cesare Borgia in *The Prince*. Machiavelli met him during two diplomatic missions, in June and October 1502. His diplomatic reports clearly indicate that he was very impressed by the duke's qualities as a leader engaged in the foundation of new political orders. The duke, Machiavelli writes,

is most splendid and magnificent and is so vigorous in military matters that there is no undertaking so great that it does not seem a minor thing to him, and he never ceases from seeking glory or enlarging his state, and he fears no effort or danger: he arrives in a place before it has been noticed that he set out from another; his soldiers love him; he has recruited the best men in

Figure 11. Altobello dei Meloni, *Caesar Borgia*, ca. 1520, oil on wood, 56 × 47 cm. Accademia Carrara, Bergamo, Italy. Photo: Erich Lessing / Art Resource, NY.

Italy: and all of this makes him victorious and formidable, to which we should add that he is perpetually lucky.[12]

Equally extraordinary was the duke's mastery at showing off his power, as the execution of his lieutenant Remirro de Orro exemplifies:

Messer Ramiro was found to-day cut into two pieces in the public square, and his body still remains there, so that the whole population has been able to see it. The

cause of his death is not precisely known, other than that
it was the pleasure of his Excellency thus to show that he
has the power to make and unmake men at his will, and
according to their merits.[13]

Some ten years later in *The Prince*, Machiavelli describes
the same episode, but this time he presents it as an example
of the Duke's extraordinary ability to gain his subjects' loyalty through an impressive staging:

> Because he realized that the rigorous measures of the
> past had generated a certain amount of hatred, in order
> to purge the minds of the people and to win them com-
> pletely over to his side he wanted to show that, if any
> form of cruelty had occurred, it did not originate from
> him but from the violent nature of his minister. Having
> found the occasion to do so, one morning at Cesena he
> had Messer Remirro's body laid out in two pieces on the
> piazza, with a block of wood and a bloody sword beside
> it. The ferocity of such a spectacle left the population
> satisfied and stupefied at the same time.

With his typical intellectual audacity, Machiavelli then
proceeds to propose the duke as a model new prince:

> Therefore, having summarized all the Duke's actions, I
> would not know how to reproach him. On the contrary,
> I believe I am correct in proposing that he be imitated by
> all those who have risen to power through the Fortune
> and with the troops of others. Possessing great courage
> and high goals, he could not have conducted himself in

any other manner, and his plans were frustrated solely by
the brevity of Alexander's life [Pope Alexander VI, father of the duke] and by his own illness. Anyone, therefore, who considers it necessary in his newly acquired
principality to protect himself from enemies, to win al-
lies, to conquer either by force or by deceit, to make himself loved and feared by the people, to be followed and
revered by his soldiers, to wipe out those who can or may
do you harm, to renovate ancient institutions with new
ones, to be both severe and kind, magnanimous and gen-
erous, to wipe out disloyal troops and create new ones, to
maintain alliances with kings and princes in such a way
that they must either gladly help you or injure you with
caution—that person cannot find more recent examples
than this man's deeds.[14]

Myths inspire, impel action, sustain commitment. They
are political forces. Because he is a true realist, Machiavelli creates them, when he feels inspired to and sees the
need for them. At the same time, he believes that human
beings judge political matters by looking at leaders' real
accomplishments: "In the actions of all men, and especially of princes, where there is no tribunal to which to
appeal, one must consider the final result," as he writes
in *The Prince*.[15] On the basis of the results, for instance,
Machiavelli severely evaluates the conduct of the king of
France, Louis XII, in Italy.[16] From the same perspective,
he also condemns the policy of neutrality in international
affairs.[17]

For Machiavelli to be a realist does not mean to be
either audacious or cautious, but to be wise enough as to

pursue the kind of political conduct that is in tune with the time and the context. In crazy times, a political decision that normally would be insane is in fact the right thing to do, Machiavelli wrote to Guicciardini.[18]

As he explained in a very important letter of September 1506 to Giovan Battista Soderini, very different modes of action lead to the same results, whereas identical modes of action lead to opposite outcomes. Scipio succeeded in Spain by governing his army with mildness and by giving an outstanding example of personal integrity. Hannibal succeeded in Italy by displaying on the contrary the most inhumane cruelty against his own soldiers. Had Scipio used Hannibal's methods in Spain, he would have failed. Hannibal would have met the same fate, had he behaved like Scipio. The key element to be considered in this case, and in general, Machiavelli explains, is the ability to act as the times and the mood of people requires ("riscontro").[19]

As a wise realist, Machiavelli knew that any state, be it a republic or a principality, needs good armies. "The main foundations of all states (whether they are new, old, or mixed)," he writes in *The Prince*, "are good laws and good armies. It is impossible to have good laws if good armies are lacking, and if there are good arms there must also be good laws."[20] Founders and redeemers need them even more. The lack or the inadequacy of military forces is the main cause of the defeat of unarmed prophets of political and moral reform like Savonarola.[21] If he wants to succeed, the redeemer Machiavelli invoked in the "Exhortation" must therefore have soldiers and captains totally loyal to him.

It is with the ideal of the redeemer in mind that Machiavelli conducted his well-known, and even too harsh,

Figure 12. English School, *Martyrdom of Savonarola*, 19th century, engraving. Private Collection / © Look and Learn / The Bridgeman Art Library.

denunciation of mercenary, auxiliary, and mixed troops in chapters XII–XIV of *The Prince*.[22] These sorts of armies are for him always useless and dangerous, but they are even more so for a redeemer who needs the total devotion of his soldiers. The section of *The Prince* on military matters, it is worth noting, ends with a celebration of Cyrus, one of the redeemers that Machiavelli cites both in chapter VI and in the "Exhortation." And Cyrus, Machiavelli remarked, was the example that inspired Scipio, one of the finest republican heroes, who was able to combine military skills and moral and civic virtues of the finest sort:

> But as for study, the prince must read stories and in them consider the deeds of excellent men. He must see how they conducted themselves in wars. He must examine the reasons for their victories and for their defeats, in order to avoid the latter and to imitate the former. Above all else, he must do as some eminent men before him have done, who elected to imitate someone who had been praised and honoured before them, and always keep in mind his deeds and actions: just as it is reported that Alexander the Great imitated Achilles, Caesar imitated Alexander, and Scipio imitated Cyrus. Anyone who reads the life of Cyrus written by Xenophon will realize how important in the life of Scipio such imitation was for his glory and how closely in purity, goodness, humanity and generosity Scipio conformed to those characteristics of Cyrus about which Xenophon had written.[23]

To serve the state well, armies must be composed of subjects, in the case of a principality, or of citizens, in the case of a republic. In addition, they must be formed of men who fear God. One of the most serious vices of mercenary armies—in addition to the fact that they are "disunited, ambitious, undisciplined and disloyal," brave with their friends, cowards with their enemies, have no faith with men—that Machiavelli mentions in *The Prince* is that "they have no fear of God." Soldiers who do not fear God cannot take a serious oath, and if they do not take the oath, they cannot be good soldiers.[24] That is why Machiavelli wanted the Florentine militia he labored so hard to create to take a solemn oath:

> This commissioner, or any deputy as described above, should the following morning, as agreed the previous day, have a solemn mass of the Holy Ghost said in such a place that all those assembled can hear it. And after this mass has been celebrated, the deputy should speak to them such words as are appropriate in such a ceremony; then he should read to them the regulations and duties that they must observe, and administer a solemn oath to them to that effect, causing each of them, one by one, to place his hand on the book of the Holy Gospels. And before they swear that oath he should read to them all the capital penalties to which they will be subject, and all the admonitions ordained by said officials in the preservation and reinforcement of their union and oath; rendering more majestic the oath with all the obligatory words of body and soul that are found to be most effective; once this has been done, they will all be free to go back to their own homes.[25]

While the fear of God is always indispensable in order to have effective armies, in the case of the redeemer it becomes absolutely necessary. As Machiavelli stresses in the "Exhortation," the redeemer counts on God's help. How would God possibly help soldiers who do not fear him?

Machiavelli also believed, however, that military might is not just a matter of troops, weapons, and strategy.[26] In addition to military power, there is the power of words. In

The Art of War, he stressed the importance of eloquence and listed rhetorical skills as one of the essential features of the good general: "To persuade or dissuade a few about a thing is very easy, because if words are not enough, you can use authority and force; but the difficulty is to remove from a multitude a belief that is unfavorable either to the common good or to your belief, when you can use only words proper to be heard by all, since you are trying to persuade them all."[27] Held in the greatest respect by ancient generals, oratory has become in modern times "completely obsolete," Machiavelli sadly remarked. And yet, nothing is more effective than eloquence, to impel an army's will, and to move the soldiers passions:

> For there are countless times when things come up by which an army would be ruined if the general either could not or was not accustomed to speak to it; this speaking lightens fear, sets courage afire, increases determination, uncovers deception, promises rewards, shows perils and the way to escape them, reproaches, begs, threatens, fills with hope, praises, berates, and does everything through which human passions are extinguished or exited.

Hence, Machiavelli concluded, "any prince or republic intending to set up a new military establishment and bring reputation to such an army must accustom its soldiers to hearing their general speak, and must accustom its generals to speak skillfully."[28]

This piece of political wisdom is particularly important for the redeemer that Machiavelli invokes in the "Exhortation." As I have remarked, his redeemer must be an armed prophet. How could he announce the prophecy of national emancipation if not with powerful and moving words that persuade soldiers and people that he is inspired by God and can count on God's help? In *The Prince*'s redeemer, three fundamental political forces converge: military might, eloquence, and religion.

A DIFFICULT REALITY TO GRASP

The truly distinctive point of Machiavelli's realism is, however, the awareness that political reality is extremely difficult to grasp.[29] A refined work of interpretation can unveil it, but only in part, and tentatively. Machiavelli's realism must not be confused with the realism of the empirical scientist who collects precise facts and identifies general laws.[30] Even less can it be compared to the approach of the political amateur who believes that general models of political behavior might help us to understand real political life.[31] His realism was instead based on the knowledge of history and the analysis of human passions.

Scholars who regard Machiavelli as one of the founders of the modern science of politics stress that he believed that the human world, like the natural world, displays regular or recurrent features that form the basis of general laws of politics. The text most frequently cited in this regard is a passage from the *Discourses*, where he writes:

> Prudent men are wont to say—and this is not rashly or without good ground—that he who would foresee what has to be, should reflect on what has been, for everything that happens in the world at any time has genuine

resemblance to what happened in ancient times. This is due to the fact that the agents who bring such things about are men, and that men have and always have had, the same passions.[32]

The belief in the sameness of human passions over history was a common one in early-sixteenth-century Florence. However, it did not encourage at all a scientific study of politics, as we understand it. Rather, it was the premise for an interpretive work aimed at identifying the specific features of political life and events, attempting predictions, offering practical advice, and writing historical narratives based on the identification of the political actors' intentions. Francesco Guicciardini, for instance, believed that "the same things always reappear," and all events have already occurred in past times. This general assumption led him to conceive the study of politics as an effort to "recognize" things with the help of historical knowledge. Understanding political events is recognition in the literal sense: we understand things when we see them for the second time—that is, by comparing them with similar events that occurred in the past (more precisely, with events that historians tell us occurred in the past).

To identify in the available historical narrations the events that can illuminate the ones that we are witnessing or that we are about to witness is an arduous task because the faces of people and external appearances change, and so do "the names and the forms of things." The geography and alchemy of human passions and intentions is quite volatile. Hence, to apply the knowledge of past events to present political affairs it takes, as Guicciardini wrote in the *Ricordi*, a "sharp and discerning eye."[33] To understand politics is therefore a job for "prudent men," not for philosophers or scientists inclined to investigate eternal and immutable principles underneath (or above) the ever-changing flux of things.

A similar awareness inspired Machiavelli's realism. Like Guicciardini, he believed that human beings have and have always had the same passions. But he also knows that each individual has *his or her* own passions and temperament, and acts accordingly. "I believe," he wrote to Giovan Battista Soderini in 1506, "that as nature has given each man an individual face, so she has given him an individual disposition and an individual imagination. From this it results that each man conducts himself according to his disposition and his imagination."[34] A true expert of politics must therefore be capable of identifying the particular disposition and imagination of individual actors, if he or she wants to predict their behavior.

To understand political leaders' real intentions, one must be "there," or at least "close" to, the event and to the people, and to collect and review facts and information. But uncertainty as to what is really going on remains. The clouds that surround political action never go away, primarily because of the ability of political actors to deceive others (and themselves, at times). Interpretive work is valuable, but hardly conclusive. The best one can hope for is to come up with convincing stories and plausible advice that will be nonetheless questioned by others coming up with different stories and offering different counsel. Judgments about princes' actions can never be final because, as Machiavelli remarks in *The Prince*, there is no judge to whom one can appeal for a conclusive verdict ("non è iudizio da reclamare").[35]

However attentive one is to observing gestures and acts, even the smallest details, it is very hard to come close to the truth of the matter. For this reason, Machiavelli presented his views as conjectures and tentative assessments. He recognized the limits of his own capacity to understand the significance of the events that were unfolding before his eyes. On the sudden departure of French troops from Duke Valentino's headquarters in Cesena in late December 1502, for instance, he wrote that "every man is making his own castles in the air," and he confessed that "from authentic sources nothing can be extracted that seems reasonable to anyone else." Even if he has not spared himself all the efforts that were necessary "to get to the truth of the matter," the truth escaped him, or, more precisely, there was no truth there.[36]

To interpret what political actors intend to do is particularly difficult because they always cover their real plans, if they have plans. In the fifteen years that he spent in the apprenticeship of the art of the state, Machiavelli had many opportunities to appreciate this distinctive quality of princes. "As I have many times written to you," he reported, for instance, from Cesena on December 22, 1502,

> this Lord is very secretive, and I do not believe that what he is going to do is known to anybody but himself. And his chief secretaries have many times asserted to me that he does not tell them anything except when he orders it. . . . Hence I beg Your Lordships will excuse me and not impute it to my negligence if I do not satisfy Your

Lordships with information, because most of the time I
do not satisfy even myself.[37]

Some years later, he registered the same secrecy in the Emperor Maximilian and expressed again his sense of frus-
tration for his inability to attain full intelligence of the
situation and therefore to offer solid material for reliable
predictions.[38]

In addition to princes' secrecy, what makes understanding political events arduous is the princes' equally notable
ability to present their intention in the most favorable light.
Once again, the duke was a master in coloring his hostile
intentions with words full of friendship and noble purposes. As Machiavelli promptly stressed in *The Prince*, the
duke had an excellent mentor in his father, Pope Alexander VI, who "was concerned only with deceiving men, and
he always found them gullible. No man ever affirmed anything more forcefully or with stronger oaths but kept his
word less. Yet, his deceptions were always effective, because
he well understood the naivety of men."[39] So did King Ferdinand the Catholic: "one present-day ruler, whom is well
to leave unnamed, is always preaching peace and trust, although he is really very hostile to both; and if he had prac-
ticed them he would have lost either reputation or power
several times over."[40]

JUDGING BY THE EYES; JUDGING BY THE HANDS

A crucial distinction that guided Machiavelli's conception
of the study of politics was that between "judging by the
eyes" and "judging by the hands."[41] As he put it in chapter

XVIII of *The Prince*, "Men in general judge more by their eyes than their hands: everyone can see but few can feel. Everyone sees what you seem to be, few touch upon what you are. . . . For ordinary people are always taken in by appearances and by the outcome of an event. And in the world there are only ordinary people." To judge by the eyes is typical of the masses; to judge by the hands, of wise men. But what does it mean exactly to "judge by the hands" or "judge by the eyes"?

The metaphor of "judging by hands" as opposed to "judging by eyes" is reminiscent of Luigi Pulci's *Morgante* and of Poggio Bracciolini's *Facezie*: A young thrush sees tears in the eyes of a man who is killing his cage mates and believes that the man will have compassion on the remaining birds until an older bird tells him to look not at the man's eyes, but at his hands. As Poggio comments, to judge well, one must look at what people do, not at what they say.[42] Unlike the majority of men who "judge more by their eyes than their hands," the good student of politics must have ways of guarding himself from princes' deceptive skills. He cannot afford to be credulous, and to let himself be deceived by appearances or by the prince's majesty.[43] Machiavelli surely endorses the old bird's wisdom, but also knows that the meaning of man's actions is not clear at all. They must be interpreted; one must touch "who the prince is." But what precisely does it mean to be able to touch who the prince is? What is there to be "touched"?

The metaphor of touching indicates a kind of knowledge that requires closeness. It means to be able to understand the passions and humors that orient particular princes' and rulers' conduct. One is possessed by the desire of glory, another by hatred, another by desire of revenge, another by lust for money, another still by fear of losing his territory or power. Because they are moved by passions, they are likely to make mistakes, just like any other man. To assume that, as a rule, they will do what is best for their states is an absurdity that never crossed Machiavelli's mind. The discussion with Francesco Vettori on international affairs that began in March 1513 offers us a number of precise insights to illuminate Machiavelli's way of assessing the princes' behavior in *The Prince*.

As Vettori wrote to Machiavelli on March 30, 1513, things often "do not proceed according to reason," and therefore it is a vain exercise to investigate political matters and speculate solutions designed to put order in the world ("rasettare questo mondo").[44] Nonetheless, for Machiavelli, the student of political life must attempt to assess the state of the things and try to predict what political leaders are likely to do given the fact that they are—each in a different way, and each in a different way in different times— dominated, or at least affected by particular passions.

Because they are based on the interpretation of passions and humors, political predictions inevitably consist of much guessing. No political decision is immune from risks and uncertainties: "Nor should any state ever believe that it can always choose safe courses of action. On the contrary, it should recognize that they will all be risky, for we find this to be in the order of things: that whenever we try to avoid one disadvantage, we run into another. Prudence consists in knowing how to recognize the nature of disadvantages, and how to choose the least sorry one as good."[45] When he discussed with Vettori whether the alliance between

France and England struck in August 1514 was likely to last, he remarked that Henry VIII of England could break the treaty either out of fear or out of envy. But he then concluded that neither passion will be strong enough to move the king to change his alliances. He interpreted the king's intentions on the basis of a general assumption about the way in which passions operate and of his knowledge of *who* the king is.

As we have seen, Machiavelli derived many ideas in *The Prince* from political experiences. It is also true that in turn he used the ideas he developed in *The Prince* to judge political events. An example is Machiavelli's assessment of the behavior of Ferdinand the Catholic. Whereas Vettori considered the conduct of the king of Spain utterly inexplicable, Machiavelli found it perfectly consistent, given the fact that his policy had always been that of rousing "great expectations about himself, all the time keeping men's minds occupied in considering what is going to be the end of new decisions and new undertakings." The king's goal is not "a particular gain or a particular victory," but "to give himself a reputation among his people and to keep them uncertain among the great number of his affairs. Therefore he is a spirited maker of beginnings, to which he later gives the particular end that is placed before him by chance and that necessity teaches him, and up to now he has not been able to complain of his luck or of his courage."[46]

To recognize that princes' conduct is affected by passions does not mean that they behave foolishly or irrationally. However reasonable they are, still each of them is reasonable given the kind of person he is—that is, given the sort of passions that orient his choices. Uncertain as it is, the knowledge we can get by interpreting the prince's words and actions permits us to elaborate a narrative that can be a fine basis for political action. The interpretive work does not end with the prince's political choice: after the facts, the work of interpretation resumes to provide this time a plausible account of what has happened, until another narrative is proposed.

When Machiavelli asserts in *The Prince* that "in the actions of all men, and especially of princes, where there is no tribunal to which to appeal, one must consider the final result," he is telling us that political facts are by their nature subject to contrasting interpretations and assessments.[47] Since they cannot be settled on the basis of rational or empirical considerations, they inevitably originate rhetorical contests in which each contender puts forth his partisan views, and colors them with general criteria. Even time's verdict concerning princes' and kings' actions is far from being conclusive. There is still ample room for dispute and conflicting interpretations on why they did what they did, or, as Machiavelli wrote in the letter of December 10, 1513, on "the reasons for their actions ("della ragione delle loro azioni"). Out of their kindness, Machiavelli continued in the same letter, the great men of antiquity "answer me." What he means is that their works and the histories that record their actions disclose their meaning because he knows how to interrogate them. His ability in interpreting the intentions of ancient men and modern men alike is the core of his political realism. When he claims that he is a serious student of the art of the state, he means

that he believes himself to be good at identifying intentions and evaluating effects, within the inescapable limits
of interpretation.

Machiavelli's manner of theorizing about politics in *The
Prince*, and in all his political works, should be described as
a refined realism that encompasses some intellectual features that are normally associated with political idealism
and political prophecy. He regards the knowledge of political reality as the most necessary requisite for effective political action, whatever the goals that political leaders want
to attain. He also explains that in all times and all places,
individuals and ordinary people ("vulgo") judge political
leaders on the basis of the effective results of their actions.
Finally, from his earliest political writings until his last letters, he insists on the necessity for any state to have a strong
and reliable military power.

All these elements of his political thought do situate
him within the tradition of political realism. Yet we also
find in his political thought a strong inclination to make
use of political imagination, in the sense that he was keen
and able to imagine political possibilities, like the redemption of Italy, that were very remote from reality (if not impossible). Not only did he believe that they could become
true, but he also dedicated his best energies, for all his life,
to make them happen. For him, political reality was made
of many elements: passions, interests, intentions, and the
ability to simulate and dissimulate. More than a system of
facts, it is a world of uncertain and ambivalent signs, words,
and gestures, accessible, only in part, through a work of interpretation. He was not at all the forerunner of the view
that politics is knowledge of reality and adaptation to it, but

a writer who imagined for his country a very different reality and wanted to contribute to create it. Without political power, without an army, Machiavelli could rely only on the power of his words. In *The Prince* and in particular in the "Exhortation," he used this power in the most impressive way, as I will discuss in the next chapter.

CHAPTER THREE

A Great Oration

A STUDENT OF RHETORIC

Machiavelli composed *The Prince* to give life, with his words, to a redeemer capable of arousing "obstinate faith," and "piety," and to revive the "ancient valor" in the hearts of the Italians. He had in mind similar goals when he set down to write the *Discourses on Livy*. He was hoping to shape the "spirits" of youths in order to encourage them to eschew their own times, filled with "every extreme misery, infamy, and reproach," and to emulate the times of antiquity, so filled with virtue and religion. In *The Art of War*, he wanted to encourage his contemporaries and posterity to "bring back" the militia into its ancient orders and to rediscover the age-old virtue. He lamented the fact that he himself was unable to undertake the work of redemption and hoped that others, in a new age, might be able to implement his teaching. All his greatest works were designed to shape souls, to teach, to revive forgotten ways of life, and to bring back dead ideas and principles. He wrote to persuade. For this reason, he composed all his political and historical works in accordance with the rules of classical rhetoric.

Figure 13. Giorgio Vasari, *Antonio Giacomini Preaching in Favor of a War against Pisa*. Detail from the ceiling in the Salone de' Cinquecento. Salone de' Cinquecento, Palazzo Vecchio, Florence, Italy. Alinari / Art Resource, NY.

Machiavelli studied the art of rhetoric from his earliest education. Classical works on rhetoric circulated in his house. "I here record," wrote Bernardo Machiavelli, Niccolò's father, "that today, December 16, 1479, I returned to Matteo the stationer the *Rhetorica ad Herennium* by Tully [Cicero] that he lent me several days back, and also I returned to Zanobi the stationer Tully's *De Oratore* that he lent me several days ago."[1] He refined his mastery of eloquence later in his life when he served the Republic as Segretario. His duties included writing official letters and composing political orations, two assignments that required excellent rhetorical skills.

He was expected to use eloquence also in diplomatic missions, when he had to persuade rulers and princes. The instructions for the legation to Caterina Sforza, dated July 12, 1499, for instance, contain these explicit guidelines:

> Upon these several points you will enlarge in the most effective language and in the best terms that may suggest themselves to you; so as to convince Her Excellency of our sincere desire for an opportunity to benefit him [the son of Caterina Sforza, Ottaviano Riario], and to acknowledge the services which he has rendered to our republic, as also of our entire confidence in him. At the same time, you will point out the necessity of the union of our states, employing the most acceptable language in your endeavor to persuade him to that effect.[2]

For the mission in France the instructions of the Signoria, dated July 18, 1500, contained even more specific recommendations concerning the rhetorical devices that Machiavelli should use. When you address the king of France or his counselors, the Signoria urged, you must resort to the of *amplificatio* and *extenuatio*. The *extenuatio* helps to attenuate our responsibilities concerning matters or events that could prove damaging, while the *amplificatio* helps to aggrandize our merits or the value of the cause that we are defending. "It will, furthermore, be proper for you to speak of the capture of our commissioner," the letter states, "of the persons guilty of this outrage, and of the manner in which it was done, and of the violence and insults we have had to bear, even from the lowest private soldier. In fact, you must make a summary of all these matters, which will go to prove that we have been treated by them more like enemies than friends, amplifying or extenuating these matters as will best serve our cause."[3]

The Signori of Florence used this language because they were aware that Machiavelli knew well the rules of rhetoric and was capable of wisely putting them into practice. We know from Machiavelli's and Francesco della Casa's reports that they diligently followed the Signoria's advice. In fact, they greatly overstated the misbehavior of the French army in the failure of the military operations against Pisa, and astutely attenuated Florentines' guilt: "We said that your Lordships had never failed to furnish the most abundant supply of provisions, and that there never had been any deficiency, but that they had been wantonly wasted, and that those who had brought them into camp had been overwhelmed with all sorts of insults and bad treatment."[4]

An even more impressive document, in this respect, is the commission that Marcello Virgilio Adriani, secretary of the first chancellery and teacher of eloquence at the Studio Fiorentino, wrote to Machiavelli explaining the rhetorical techniques to employ with Giampagolo Baglioni, tyrant of Perugia. Machiavelli should open his speech with words designed to put Baglioni in a well-disposed state. He should then arrange the order of his arguments in accordance with the technique of the *dispositio*[5] and above all, be sure to use the commonplace that the reputation of being an ingrate is very harmful for a prince. Last, he should

employ amplification and extenuation so as to move the
interlocutor to reveal his inner thoughts: "You will shape
your remarks to him in such a wise manner as to make it
appear that this is the only object of your mission"; you
must then "stir [Baglioni] up in some way," explaining to
him the blame that will fall on him for "the ingratitude that
may be imputed to him for all the benefits he has received
in the past, and his want of faith as a soldier, the two essential and fundamental points that men look to"; finally, "you
must endeavor to remove the apprehensions which he pre-
tends to have," and "you must try to bring him to the point
of revealing to you the real motive for his determination."[6]

Machiavelli's solid mastery of rhetoric is even more
evident in the speeches he composed during his years as
secretary. One example is the oration entitled *Parole da
dirle sopra la provisione del danaio, facto un poco di proemio
et di scusa* (*Words to Be Spoken on the Law for Appropriating Money, after Giving a Little Introduction and Excuse*),
which he wrote probably for the lifetime Gonfalonier Pier
Soderini in March 1503 to persuade the Great Council—
the highest legislative body of the Republic—to approve
new taxes needed to provide Florence with the armies necessary for its defense. He opens the oration by stating a
commonly held general principle:

> all the cities that ever at any time have been ruled by an
> absolute prince, by aristocrats or by the people, as is this
> one, have had for their protection force combined with
> prudence, because the latter is not enough alone, and the
> first either does not produce things or, when they are
> produced, does not maintain them. Force and prudence,

then, are the might of all the governments that ever have been or will be in the world. Hence any man who has considered change of kingdoms and the destruction of provinces and of cities has not seen them caused by anything other than failure in arms or in good sense.

Having set forth the fundamental principle on which his whole argument rested, Machiavelli proceeded to refute the belief of the citizens of Florence that, in case of danger, the king of France would hasten to the city's rescue. To move the Florentines away from this dangerous but deeply rooted opinion, Machiavelli resorted to another general principle of political wisdom, soundly corroborated by history: "Every city, every state ought to consider as enemies all those who can hope to take possession of her territory and against whom she cannot defend herself. Never was a princedom or republic wise that was willing to let her territory stand in the power of others or which, so letting it stand, thought she held it securely." To make that same concept more evident and persuasive, he resorted to an image: "It is not always possible to put your hand on another's sword, and therefore it is good to have a sword at your side and to gird it on when the enemy is at a distance, because afterward it is too late and you have no recourse."

After having used rational considerations, Machiavelli tries to win over the audience by touching their passions, in this case the fear of violent death. To this effect he narrates a terrifying story that the Florentines remembered well:

Many of you can remember when Constantinople was taken by the Turks. That Emperor foresaw his ruin. He

called upon his citizens, not being able with his organized forces to make proper provision. He showed them
their dangers, showed them the preventives, and they
ridiculed him. The siege came on. Those citizens who
had before had no respect for the exhortations of their
lord, when they heard within their walls the thunder
of the artillery and the yells of the army of their enemies, ran weeping to the Emperor with their bosoms
full of money; but he drove them away, saying: "Go to
die with this money, since you have not wished to live
without it."

The exhortation that ends the speech appeals instead
to his fellow-citizens' deep-rooted pride in their liberty:
"Such a fall I cannot believe in, when I see that you are free
Florentines and that in your own hands rests your liberty.
For that liberty I believe you will have such regards as they
always have had who are born free and hope to live free."[7]

An Example of Deliberative Rhetoric

It is in *The Prince*, however, that Machiavelli best displayed
his mastery of rhetoric. This time, he wants to persuade everyone that he knows the art of the state better than anyone
else. He also wants to give life to a founder and a redeemer.
To achieve these goals he needed to write a great oration
in full compliance with the rules of the deliberative genre
of rhetoric.

The dedicatory letter to Lorenzo de' Medici serves as
a preamble, and as such it is intended to render the reader

well-disposed, docile, and benevolent. Had he dedicated
the letter to Giuliano de' Medici, as he considered doing, or
to anyone else, the structure would probably have been the
same. Machiavelli emphasized here his own good qualities: his experience, his knowledge of affairs of state, the
sacrifices that he has had to make to gain his knowledge
of statecraft, and the bad fortune that prevented him from
receiving adequate recognition. He wrote, in fact, that he
has condensed in this book "the knowledge of the actions
of great men, learned by me from long experience with
modern things and a continuous reading of ancient ones,"
attained "in so many years and with so many hardships and
dangers."

To make the reader well-disposed to accept his advice
and his exhortations, Machiavelli tried also to remove the
doubts or hostile opinions concerning his own person and
his authority in providing political counsel—in particular,
the prejudice, which was current in the Florence of his time,
that a man who did not belong to the political elite could
not properly discuss affairs of state with princes, and that
such a privilege was exclusively the domain of powerful and
wealthy citizens. To challenge this belief he stresses that
he is in fact in a better position to give advice on political
matters: "To know well the nature of people one needs to
be prince, and to know well the nature of princes one needs
to be of the people."

To further enhance his credibility, he openly proclaims
his loyalty to the house of Medici: "Therefore, your Magnificence, take this small gift in the spirit with which I send
it. If your Magnificence considers and reads it diligently,

you will learn from it my extreme desire that you arrive at the greatness that fortune and your other qualities promise you." Nor did he miss the opportunity, counseled by the classics, to point out that he has suffered although innocent and that his merits have been overlooked: "And if your Magnificence will at some time turn your eyes from the summit of your height to these low places, you will learn how undeservedly I endure a great and continuous malignity of fortune."

His assertion in the dedicatory letter that he has not filled his book "with fulsome phrases nor with pompous and magnificent words, nor with any blandishment or superfluous ornament whatever," has been interpreted as compelling evidence that Machiavelli did reject rhetoric. In fact, it reveals that he was wisely and diligently applying the rules of deliberative rhetoric. The Roman masters had in fact explained that an oration of the deliberative genre should be in a simple and grave style ("simplex et gravis"), because the material under discussion itself possessed magnificence and splendor.[8] Machiavelli tells us that "I wanted it either not to be honored for anything or to please solely for the variety of the matter and the gravity of the subject."[9]

The simple and grave style requires, however, appropriate ornaments designed to make an orator's discourse clear and persuasive. Inspiring examples taken from history are especially effective.

Machiavelli's examples, it must be stressed, are not scientific, but rhetorical. They do not serve the purpose of demonstrating the empirical validity of a scientific law, but to render more persuasive a piece of political advice and to stimulate the desire to emulate a specific way of acting.[11]

Other useful rhetorical devices are similes, images, and metaphors, which Machiavelli employs as well. To explain that a new prince should be capable of using both force and deceit, he chooses the images of the fox and the lion: "Thus, since a prince is compelled of necessity to know well how to use the beast, he should pick the fox and the lion, because the lion does not defend itself from snares and the fox does not defend itself from wolves. So one needs to be a fox to recognize snares and a lion to frighten the wolves."[12]

Less famous, but equally in accordance with rhetorical techniques, is his use of a "figure" of the Old Testament: "When David offered to Saul to go and fight Goliath, the Philistine challenger, Saul, to give him spirit, armed him with his own arms—which David, as soon as he had them on, refused, saying that with them he could not give a good account of himself, and so he would rather meet the enemy with his sling and his knife."[13] As he stated in the *Discourses*, Machiavelli read the Bible "judiciously";[14] he meant to say that he was interested in extracting from the text useful political advice.[15] From the story of David's gesture, he derives the teaching "the arms of others fall off your back or weigh you down or hold you tight."[16]

Machiavelli also resorts to the technique of irony as a means of derision to belittle and censure. One example is the chapter on ecclesiastic principalities, where he wrote that those states maintain themselves without virtue and without fortune,

> for they are sustained by orders that have grown old with religion, which have been so powerful and of such a kind that they keep their princes in the state however they proceed and live. These alone have states, and do not defend them; they have subjects, and do not govern them and the states though undefended are not taken from them; the subjects, though ungoverned, do not care, and they neither think of becoming estranged from such princes nor can they. Thus, only these principalities are secure and happy. But as they subsist by superior causes, to which the human mind does not reach, I will omit speaking of them; for since they are exalted and maintained by God, it would be the office of a presumptuous and foolhardy man to discourse on them.[17]

What he really meant was that ecclesiastical princes deserve to lose their states, and will lose them, even if they proclaim that they derive their power from God, because they do not govern their subjects in the right manner.[18]

The subdivision of *The Prince* too follows the rules of deliberative rhetoric. After the dedicatory letter that serves as an *exordium* (introduction), Machiavelli inserts a proper *partition* (outline), in which he concisely explains to the reader the subject matter of his oration: "I shall leave out reasoning on republics because I have reasoned on them at length another time. I shall address myself only to the principality, and shall proceed by weaving together the threads mentioned above; and I shall debate how these principalities may be governed and maintained."[19] He then defines the various sorts of principalities ("How many kinds of principalities there are and the ways they are acquired"; "Of hereditary principalities"; "Of mixed principalities") and the different ways through which they are founded and governed.

At the center of *The Prince* Machiavelli puts the political and moral points he wanted to sustain, and criticizes the views he intended to defeat. It is in fact in chapters XII to XVIII that he discussed his fundamental claims on military matters and political ethics. The meaning of these much debated chapters becomes clear if we consider the indications that the Latin masters of eloquence had taught the proper aims of political advising. The most relevant source for Machiavelli on this subject was the *Rhetorica ad Herennium*. The author of this text teaches that the goal of the good orator addressing political issues ("in civili consultatione") should only be interest. It also teaches, and this is an important point, that interest ("utilitas") consists of two parts: security ("tuta") and honesty ("honestas").[20] Then he subdivides security into might and craft ("vim et dolum"). "Might is determined by armies, fleets, arms, engines of war, recruiting of man power, and the like"; craft "is exercised by means of money, promises, dissimulation, swiftness, deception." Honesty is subdivided into the right and the praiseworthy ("rectum et laudabile"). "The Right is that which is done in accord with Virtue and Duty. Subheads under the Right are Wisdom, Justice, Courage, and Temperance." On the other hand, "The Praiseworthy is what produces an honorable remembrance, at the time of the event and afterwards."[21]

Machiavelli flatly asserts that the overarching goal of *The Prince* is to counsel what is useful to a new prince ("my intent is to write something useful to whoever understands it").[22] But by "utility" he meant, as the *Ad Herennium* had instructed, security (understood as force and cunning) and honesty (that which is praiseworthy and virtuous).[23] In chapter XXIV, in fact, Machiavelli explicitly referred to security as one of the purposes of his advice, while in chapter XVIII he insisted upon honor and praise: "So let a prince win and maintain his state: the means will always be judged honorable, and will be praised by everyone." The issue of esteem and reputation emerges also in chapter XXI, where Machiavelli stressed that a prince must devote his best energies to acquire esteem and to this effect he must be a lover of the virtues, protect his subjects, allow them to pursue their activities in tranquility, and be sure that "no one should be afraid to increase his property for fear that it will be taken away from him." As for virtue, he stated (chapter XV) that his advice is in keeping with virtue, even if it appears to be vice. He recommended what is just in the "Exhortation": "Their undertaking was not more just than this one, nor easier. . . . Here there is great justice: 'For war is just to whom it is necessary.'"

The other two fundamental components of utility in deliberative rhetoric, force and cunning, are analyzed in detail in chapters XII to XIV and in chapter XVIII, respectively. On force, as I have already mentioned, Machiavelli stressed that mercenary, auxiliary, and mixed troops are useless and dangerous and that a new prince "must not have any other object nor any other thought, nor must adopt anything as his art but war, its institutions, and its discipline; because that is the only art befitting one who commands." On cunning and simulation, he did not hesitate to write that the princes who have accomplished great things "have thought little about keeping faith and have known how cunningly to manipulate men's minds," and that "a prince must be very careful never to let anything fall from his lips that is not imbued with the five qualities mentioned above; to those seeing and hearing him, he should appear to be all mercy, all faithfulness, all integrity, all humanity, and all religion."

When he discussed in *The Prince* the contrast between what is useful and what is honest, Machiavelli intended to intervene in Florentine debates on matters of domestic and international politics, rather than attack advice books for princes.[24] The issue was in fact frequently debated in Florentine councils and advisory bodies. Piero Aldobrandini, for instance, speaking during a discussion on foreign affairs, emphasized that "it is best not to break promises made to the Most Christian [King of France], because it has always been an ancient tradition of this Republic not to break our word to others." In the same debate, Bono Boni exhorted the Ten of Liberty to keep the promises that they had made "because, this city has never broken its word to anyone, and that he would rather die altogether than break his word, because at least that would be a great-spirited death."[25] Another orator reiterated the same point of view: "Those forefathers of mine . . . always held the same determination, that once you made a promise, you must keep it, indeed, even if it might be dangerous; from which maxim I do not wish at all to vary, because honesty should be put before utility, if necessity, which obeys no law, did not compel us to act otherwise."[26]

Other members of the Florentine élite were, however, of the opposite view and held that there are cases in which utility comes before honesty. Their arguments were consistent with fifteenth-century political theorists who wrote on civic ethos. A faithful follower of Cicero, Matteo Palmieri, wrote for instance that

> the truth approved by the greatest minds and by the authority of stern and grave philosophers in no way divides or separates honesty from utility, indeed, it joins them together; and they insist that that which is honest must also be useful, and that which is useful must also be honest, nor do they admit in any way that the two qualities be divided: the wisdom of which is certainly approved and true. But matters are judged otherwise when in disputation the truth itself is examined more closely, and otherwise do words find application in the common opinion of the great masses. To us, speaking at present in the vernacular, it is fitting to employ words in accordance with the usage of the common folk, and to leave aside the well honed subtleties of absolute truth. And as the many say, so shall we, at times something that is not honest may be useful, and something that is not useful may be honest.[27]

There is no doubt that *The Prince* sustained the views of those who maintained that there are circumstances in which utility and safety must be put before honesty. In the central section of his work—chapters XV to XVIII—Machiavelli openly rejected the Ciceronian doctrine that what is useful is also honest and that what is honest is also useful. In particular, he used the argument of necessity in chapter XV: "Hence it is necessary to a prince, if he wants to maintain himself, to learn to be able not to be good and to use this and not use it according to necessity"; and in chapter XVIII:

> This has to be understood: that a prince, and especially a new prince, cannot observe all those things for which men are held good, since he is often under a necessity, to maintain his state, of acting against faith, against charity, against humanity, against religion. And so he needs to have a spirit disposed to change as the winds of fortune and variations of things command him, and as I said above, not depart from good, when possible, but know how to enter in evil, when forced by necessity.

In chapter XV, probably following the *Ad Herennium*,[28] he makes the same point using the technique of redescribing the meaning of words:[29] "And furthermore one should not care about incurring the reputation of those vices without which it is difficult to save one's state; for if one considers everything well, one will find something appears to be virtue, which if pursued would be one's ruin, and something else appears to be vice, which if pursued results in one's security and well-being."[30]

Were it a treatise designed to instruct a new prince on the most effective ways to consolidate his power, *The Prince* would have ended with chapter XXIV where Machiavelli asserts: "When the things written above have been observed prudently, they make a new prince appear ancient and immediately render him more secure and steady in his state than if he had grown old in it." But since Machiavelli was writing for a redeemer, he needed an inspiring conclusion.

THE PROPHECY OF *THE PRINCE*

The Prince's last two chapters are designed to persuade the reader that emancipatory political action is possible and that those who commit themselves to it attain true and lasting glory. In chapter XXV ("Of Fortune's power in human affairs and how she can be resisted"), Machiavelli refuted the view that "the affairs of this world are dominated by Fortune and by God, that men cannot control them with their prudence, and that, on the contrary, men can have no remedy whatsoever for them," and affirmed that "in order not to wipe out our free will, I consider it to be true that Fortune is the arbiter of one half of our actions, but that she still leaves the control of the other half, or almost that, to us."[31]

As he had done in the previous chapters, he conveyed his points with impressive images. First, he presented fortune as a violent river that can however be restrained by human prudence and virtue. Then, to urge a possible redeemer to be prepared to act with the utmost determination and courage, he resorted to the metaphor of fortune as woman:

I therefore conclude that, since Fortune varies and men remain obstinate in their ways, men prosper when the two are in harmony and fail to prosper when they are not in accord. I certainly believe this: that it is better to be impetuous than cautious, because Fortune is a woman, and if you want to keep her under it is necessary to beat her and to force her down. It is clear that she more often allows herself to be won over by impetuous men than by those who proceed coldly. And so, like a woman, Fortune is always the friend of young men, for they are less cautious, more ferocious, and command her with more audacity.

It is, however, in the final chapter—the "Exhortation"— that Machiavelli employed the whole range of rhetorical devices apt to touch the passions that impel men to act. Some scholars have judged it to be useless, harmful, unsuccessful, and poorly linked to the rest of the work. It is, instead, a perfect conclusion to the text.[32] The rules of classical rhetoric in fact prescribe that, for a political oration to be persuasive, it must end, after a brief summation of the theses put forth, with a *peroratio* (conclusion) or an *exhortatio* (exhortation) in which the orator touches the passions of the listeners to move them to decide or act in accordance with his advice. In order to achieve this goal, the orator must use above all the techniques of *indignatio* (indignation), in order to arouse disdain in his listeners, and *conquestio* (lamentation), in order to arouse compassion.[33] In the first case, he must emphasize that the actions he is denouncing are grim, cruel, nefarious, and tyrannical;[34] in the second case, he must insist especially upon the innocence and the weakness of the victim.[35] To move a potential redeemer to indignation, he stressed the "barbarous cruelties and insults"; in order to arouse compassion, he described Italy as "more enslaved than the Hebrews, more servile than the Persians, more dispersed than the Athenians: without a head, without order, beaten, despoiled, torn, pillaged, and having endured ruin of every sort."

To give his words even more persuasive power, Machiavelli stressed that the whole enterprise would be just ("this is a righteous cause") and unproblematic:

> Nor can I express with what love he will be received in all those territories that have suffered through those foreign floods; with what thirst for revenge, with what stubborn loyalty, with what devotion, with what tears! What doors will be closed to him? What people will deny him their obedience? What envy could oppose him? What Italian could deny him homage?

In addition to the people's love, the redeemer can count on the help of God himself, the God of the Exodus who loves justice and a civil way of life, and therefore is the friend of those who want to found and reform states and redeem people. The signs of the friendship of God were evident, especially in the case of Moses: "Here may be seen extraordinary things without example, brought about by God: the sea has opened; a cloud has escorted you along the way; the stone has poured forth water; here manna has rained." *The Prince* ends with Machiavelli's silence. He preferred to let Petrarch announce the prophecy of the rebirth of virtue and the redemption of Italy because he believed, as I have stressed, that "many times poets are filled with divine and prophetic spirit."[36]

The myth of resurrection and rebirth that has inspired all Machiavelli's political works. In *The Blessed Spirits* (*Canto degli spiriti beati*), probably composed in March 1513, just before he sat down to work on *The Prince*, Machiavelli referred to the myth of the return of the golden age and the revival of ancient virtue with words similar, once again, to those of Petrarch:

> Oh, throw away all fear,
> All enmity and hate.
> All greed and pride and cruelty away!
> And in your hearts once more
> Let love of true and noble virtue rise,
> And bring the world back to that ancient day.
> This is the only way
> To open up a path to paradise
> Where flame of valor never dies.[37]

In the *Discourses on Livy*, written to resurrect in the spirit of young Italians Roman republican wisdom and virtue, he dedicated to the idea of rebirth a whole chapter in which he explained that republics and principalities can be resurrected by the simple virtue of one man.[38] In the *Art of War* (1521), he remarked that Italy seems to "be made to revive the dead things of the past."[39] But his tone here is disconsolate. He gives the impression of writing to keep alive an idea, rather than to impel action. In *The Prince*, instead, he writes of the redemption of Italy with the hope of making it possible and of actively contributing to it. It took a long time for readers to grasp *The Prince*'s message of redemption, but eventually this message was able to inspire and move, and to become a powerful political and moral force, as I will document in the next and last chapter.

CHAPTER FOUR

A Prophet of Emancipation

An Unheard Voice

The interpretation of *The Prince* as a text on political redemption has a long and fascinating history, although much less studied in comparison with the readings of Machiavelli's treatise as a theory of statecraft independent from ethics, or as the foundation of modern political science, or as a disguised book for republicans. What follows is only a partial reconstruction of the impact of the myth of the redeemer that Machiavelli designed in *The Prince*.

In Machiavelli's lifetime, and for many years to come, until the late eighteenth century, his invocation of a redeemer had no intellectual or political impact. As Hegel wrote in his essay *The Constitution of Germany* (1803?), "Machiavelli's voice has died away without effect." In the sixteenth and seventeenth centuries, political theorists, theologians, philosophers, and pamphleteers vehemently attacked *The Prince* as a handbook for tyrants and as the wicked work of a man dedicated to the purpose of detaching political action from Christian ethics. The promoters of this line of attack against *The Prince* that culminated, but did not end, with the inscription, in 1559 in the *Index of Prohibited Books*, were not interested at all in the theme of the redeemer and paid almost no attention to the "Exhortation."[1]

Equally uninterested were the political philosophers who rewrote or interpreted *The Prince* from an academic perspective. The most eloquent example is Agostino Nifo, who revised Machiavelli's text with the title *De Regnandi Peritia* (Naples, 1523), with the evident goal of composing a respectable work along the classical guidelines of Aristotle's *Politics*. While he was able to insert in his essay, in a different order and with considerable amendments and corrections, all the chapters of *The Prince*, Nifo completely ignored the last two, XXV and XXVI, as if they did not exist. Philosophical considerations aside, Machiavelli's "Exhortation to liberate Italy" would have been utterly out of place in a book dedicated to Charles V, the real dominator, directly or indirectly, of Italy.[2]

A few timid signs of the circulation of Machiavelli's ideas on founders are visible in the philosopher and physician Girolamo Cardano's *De Sapientia* (1544). In this work, Cardano indicated as appropriate examples of the power of wisdom in political affairs the rare and marvelous men that Machiavelli had cited in chapter VI of *The Prince*: Moses, Cyrus, Romulus, and Theseus. Three of them, Cardano stressed, had been exposed when they were infants and then rescued: a clear evidence of their divine origin and of God's friendship to them. He also mentioned the unarmed prophets who failed, like Savonarola, to attain their goals of redemption and noted that Machiavelli surely considered Christ too an unarmed prophet but did not dare to explicitly include his name in the list because he was too honest to do so ("propter honestatem"). As for the armed prophets like Moses, Cyrus, Romulus, and Theseus, their political triumphs are a clear indication that wisdom, or virtue, can win over fortune. Even if Cardano accepted some of Machiavelli's themes and ideas, he did not grasp nor appreciate *The Prince*'s message about founders. In particular, he did not endorse at all the passion and the will to redeem Italy that sustains the "Exhortation." He lamented the ineptitude of Italian princes who owed their power to fortune and not to their virtue, but he quietly acquiesced to Charles V's triumph.[3]

Even the political writers who praised Machiavelli as a republican thinker paid little attention to the myth of the founder and the redeemer. An eloquent example is Albericus Gentili, a jurist educated at Perugia who fled to England and was appointed in 1587 Regius Professor of civil law in Oxford. In his *De Legationibus*, issued in 1585, he wrote a eulogy of Machiavelli to laud him as the author of the golden ("aureas") observations on Livy, and as a man of unique prudence and learning. Those who have written against him, Gentili claimed, have not understood his ideas at all. The truth is that Machiavelli was

> a strong supporter and enthusiast for democracy. [He] was born, educated and received public honours in a Republic. He was extremely hostile to tyranny. Therefore he did not help the tyrant; his intention was not to instruct the tyrant, but by making all his secrets clear and openly displaying the degree of wretchedness to the people

while appearing to instruct the prince he was actually educating the people.[4]

In this strong and highly influential republican rehabilitation of Machiavelli, however, there is no mention at all of the prince as a founder.

The Machiavellian myth of the founder timidly surfaced in the context of the English Revolution when a fair number of political writers regarded the Lord protector Oliver Cromwell as the true example of a Machiavellian new prince, dedicated, like Moses, Cyrus, Romulus, and Theseus, to the most arduous task of founding new and just political orders.[5] An example is the *Horatian Ode* composed by Andrew Marvell shortly after May 1650, when Cromwell returned in triumph from Ireland, where he had crushed the rebellion there. Like Machiavelli's founder, Marvell depicted Oliver Cromwell as a man capable of creating a new state to replace old political orders. Unlike tyrants who are possessed by political ambition, Cromwell was for Marvell a founder inspired by a genuine commitment to the public good. The new Moses that Machiavelli had invoked seemed to have appeared, not in Italy, but in England.[6]

Machiavelli's ideas about founders are only marginally present in one of the most "Machiavellian" republican political tracts of the seventeenth century, James Harrington's *Oceana* (1656). Harrington regarded Machiavelli as the only modern political writer to have rediscovered the "ancient prudence" revealed to humanity "by God himself" in order to establish and preserve governments founded on the common interest and the rule of law.[7] Harrington believed that the republic is the kingdom of Christ and the true manifestation of divinity on earth. He merged into a single concept the ideal of the good citizen derived from Roman political thought and the ideal of the good Christian taken from the Bible. In his praise, Harrington went as far as to write that Machiavelli was a thinker who followed in the footsteps of Moses. He meant to say that Machiavelli was a republican theorist who rediscovered the wisdom that inspired Moses to establish the Commonwealth of Israel.[8]

Harrington also embraced the view—which Machiavelli had explained in the *Discourses on Livy*, I, 9—that founders of new political orders must have absolute power to be able to accomplish their high goal, and must be excused if they have to resort to extraordinary means, as Romulus did. This Machiavellian principle was sustained by the great patriot Olphaus Megaletor, who became Lord Archon, the sole legislator of Oceana, through which it is easy to recognize Oliver Cromwell:

> For the first, it is certain, says Machiavel, that a commonwealth is seldom or never well turned or constituted, except it has been the work of one man; for which cause a wise legislator, and one whose mind is firmly set, not upon private but the public interest, not upon his posterity but upon his country, may justly endeavor to get the sovereign power into his own hands; nor shall any man that is master of reason blame such extraordinary means as in that case will be necessary, the end proving no other than the constitution of a well-order'd commonwealth.[9]

Harrington's sole legislator and wise architect are, however, different from Machiavelli's founder. The former are great men who operate in a political world in which God does not intervene; the latter is sent by God and accomplishes his great goal through God's friendship. While Machiavelli's founder is a follower of Moses, the figure that Harrington took up from his writings, and proposed to English republican theorists and militants, is instead Romulus, the founder who did not recur to God's help.

While English republicans did not fully embrace the Machiavellian myth of the founder, seventeenth-century French freethinkers fiercely censured it as a shameful lie. What Machiavelli praised as a fine virtue of the founder— his ability to persuade that he is inspired by God—was judged by the freethinkers and the libertines as a vicious simulation. The anonymous author of the *Theophrastus redivivus* (1659), an emblematic work of seventeenth-century atheistic and materialist philosophy, described Machiavelli as the thinker who denounced Moses and Christ as impostors who used fakery to pass themselves off as gods, and who showed that all lawgiver princes are frauds and impostors ("deceptores et simulatores"), and that religion was nothing more than a gimmick and deception in the pursuit of power.[10]

The *Traité des trois imposteurs* (*Treatise of the Three Impostors: The Life and Spirit of Master Benedict Benedetto de Spinosa*), one of the most important clandestine texts of the late seventeenth century, also contains a direct attack against the myth of the divinely inspired founder. "All ancient legislators—we read—wishing to reinforce, consolidate, and establish good foundations for the laws that they were giving to their peoples, were unable to come up with anything better than to render public and claim, with all

the skills they possessed, that they had received them directly from some deity or other." While the *Traité des trois
imposteurs* considers the founders of religions to be so many
deceivers who exploit the ignorance of the people, Machiavelli placed them among men worthy of the highest praise.[11]

Another freethinker, Giulio Cesare Vanini (1585–
1619), was to a degree able to incorporate Machiavelli's
myth of the redeemer within his naturalistic interpretation of politics.[12] He believed that human history is subject
to an incessant and unstoppable cycle of corruption and
generation, without purpose and without divine guidance.
He also believed that pagan religion was very effective in
preserving and expanding the empire, not only because it
promised eternal rewards to those who died on behalf of
the fatherland, but also because it set up simple mortals as
gods to be worshipped, thereby encouraging men to act in
such a way that they might hope to rise to attain an almost
divine status. Great lawgivers could impose their laws and
emancipate people because they were armed: "Christ always found himself helpless and all those who set out to
defend the truth unarmed (says Machiavelli) died miser-
ably. Moses, on the other hand, always proceeded armed."
Machiavelli's ideal of the founder as a man of outstanding
virtue helped by God slowly begun to resurface as a myth
of political emancipation.

As is well known, Jean-Jacques Rousseau, the most
influential republican thinker of the eighteenth century,
eloquently defended Machiavelli's *Prince* by writing in
the *Contrat Social* words that became very popular among
the European learned community: "While appearing to
instruct kings he has done much to educate the people.

Machiavelli's *Prince* is the book of Republicans." On the fundamental issue of the legislator, however, Rousseau accepted Machiavelli's ideas only in part. A legislator, he wrote, in the footsteps of Plato's *Statesman*, is an individual with almost divine qualities: "a superior intelligence beholding all the passions of men without experiencing any of them." This intelligence, Rousseau continued, "would have to be wholly unrelated to our nature, while knowing it through and through; its happiness would have to be independent of us, and yet ready to occupy itself with ours; and lastly, it would have, in the march of time, to look forward to a distant glory, and, working in one century, to be able to enjoy it in the next. It would take gods to give men laws."

Like Machiavelli's great legislators of antiquity, Rousseau's ideal legislator is able to persuade his fellow citizens that he is inspired by God:

> Thus in the task of legislation we find together two things which appear to be incompatible: an enterprise too difficult for human powers, and, for its execution, an authority that is no authority. There is a further difficulty that deserves attention. Wise men, if they try to speak their language to the common herd instead of its own, cannot possibly make themselves understood. There are a thousand kinds of ideas which it is impossible to translate into popular language. . . . The legislator therefore, being unable to appeal to either force or reason, must have recourse to an authority of a different order, capable of constraining without violence and persuading without convincing. This is what has, in all ages, compelled the

fathers of nations to have recourse to divine interven-
tion and credit the gods with their own wisdom, in order
that the people, submitting to the laws of the State as to
those of nature, and recognizing the same power in the
formation of the city as in that of man, might obey freely,
and bear with docility the yoke of the public happiness.[13]

But the analogy ends here. Rousseau maintained that
the legislator credits the gods with his own wisdom; Machiavelli asserted that his founder is sent by God, succeeds
because of God's friendship, and shares with God his glory.
Rousseau too pointed to Moses as the greatest example to
follow.[14] But Rousseau's Moses is a champion of wisdom;
Machiavelli's is an armed prophet. He not only persuades
his fellows with words; he keeps them persuaded with the
sword, when they no longer believe what they must believe
if his political orders are to last.

THE *MARSEILLAISE* OF THE SIXTEENTH CENTURY

The impact of Machiavelli's ideas on founders radically
changed in a few years, between 1794 and 1808, when
three major political theorists and writers, Vittorio Alfieri,
Georg Wilhelm Friedrich Hegel, and Johann Gottlieb
Fichte, retrieved from *The Prince* the myth of the redeemer.
The much belated popularity of Machiavelli's ideas was to
a considerable degree the consequence of the emergence
of nineteenth-century movements of national emancipation and unity. In the case of Vittorio Alfieri (1749–1803),
however, the myth of the redeemer fit perfectly well with

his radical republican ideas on political liberty and with his persuasion that Christian religion could be a powerful ally of political liberty. Following the "divine Machiavelli," as he liked to call him, Alfieri called the heads of religions, the prophets, the saints, and the martyrs, "superior men" who "deserve, even from the most irreligious of men, admiration, devotion, and veneration." If we bring back religion to its founding principles, as Machiavelli had suggested, Alfieri assured us, Italians will be able to achieve the much needed moral and political regeneration.

In this spirit, Alfieri ended his work *The Prince and the Letters* with an open tribute to Machiavelli. The last chapter has in fact the same title as the last chapter of *The Prince*: "Exhortation to Free Italy from the Barbarians" ("Esortazione a liberar l'Italia dai barbari"). Italy, Alfieri stressed, can have a future as a republic, and thus become once again free and great, because there is no reason, as Machiavelli has taught us, to believe that what has been done by men in the past can no longer be achieved by other men in the present, especially on the same soil. If it will ever be able to rediscover and reexamine itself, the Italian people will surely resume a life in accordance with the principles of the true Christian religion. In Alfieri's hands, Machiavelli's "Exhortation" becomes no longer an appeal to a redeemer but the impassioned call for the moral and religious regeneration of the Italian people. The very principle of the Italian Risorgimento made, therefore, one of its earliest appearances in reflections on Machiavelli's Exhortation."[15] After almost three centuries, Machiavelli's vision of redemption began to effectively contribute to inspire Italians to commit themselves to the emancipation of their country.

In the same years, Hegel powerfully vindicated and extolled Machiavelli's myth of the redeemer in his essay on *The German Constitution* (*Die Verfassung Deutschlands*). Like Machiavelli's Italy, Hegel wrote, "Germany is no longer a state," as the wars against Napoleon have amply proved. It is like "fallen fruit [that] can be seen to have belonged to a particular tree because it lies beneath its branches; but neither its position beneath the tree nor the shade which the tree casts over it can save it from decomposition and from the power of the elements to which it now belongs."[16] It is to Machiavelli's *Prince*, Hegel stressed, that Germany must turn, if she wants to regain political unity and national dignity:

> Deeply conscious of this state of universal misery, hatred, upheaval and blindness, an Italian statesman, with cool deliberation grasped the necessary idea of saving Italy by uniting it into a single state. With rigorous logic, he mapped out the way forward which both the country's salvation and the corruption and blind folly of the age made necessary, and appealed in the following words to his prince to assume the exalted role of savior of Italy and to earn the fame of bringing its misfortune to an end.[17]

The words that Hegel cited are taken from that section of the "Exhortation" in which Machiavelli designed the image of the redeemer. Hegel remarked that from Machiavelli we must extract as an article of faith and a principle of political science the wisdom that, against the senseless clamor for so-called liberty, "freedom is possible only when a people is legally united within a state." When such a grand achievement is at stake, Hegel stressed, it is puerile to launch against Machiavelli moral platitudes such as "the end does not justify the means" for the simple reason that founders and redeemers have no choice as to the means they can use: "Gangrenous limbs cannot be cured by lavender-water, and a situation in which poison and assassination have become common weapons permits no half measures. Life which is close to decay can be reorganized only by the most drastic means."[18] Instead of condemning him as a teacher of immorality, Machiavelli must be praised as a genuinely political mind—that is, as a realist political mind that understands that "the fate of a people which rapidly approaches political destruction can be averted by a genius."[19] To have passed to future generations this jewel of political wisdom was Machiavelli's highest achievement. The essay on the *Constitution of Germany* ends on a perfect Machiavellian note, invoking a new Theseus capable of uniting Germany with force but also endowed with "enough magnanimity to grant the people he has created out of scattered groups a share in matters of common concern."[20]

A few years later, in 1807, Johann Gottlieb Fichte published in the journal *Vesta*, edited in Königsberg, an essay on Machiavelli, with a long selection from his works.[21] The essay is an important document of Fichte's political and intellectual transition from his fervent support of the French Revolution to the nationalist positions that he fully developed in the *Addresses to the German Nation* (*Reden an die deutsche Nation*, 1808), and an indication of the new interpretation of Machiavelli as a theorist of national emancipation and unity. In this sense, Fichte's essay is similar to Hegel's considerations in the *Constitution of Germany*, even if the intellectual and political focus of Fichte's analysis is the nation, while Hegel's is the state. Like Hegel, Fichte believed that Machiavelli was a political theorist who better than any other could provide precious indications for Germany's regeneration as a free nation. In this spirit, he discussed at length Machiavelli's ideas on morality, on military issues, and on religion and examined the much debated issue of the relationship between *The Prince* and the *Discourses*. The most relevant aspect of Fichte's text, for our story, however, is that he chose the "Exhortation" as the opening text of his selections from Machiavelli's works. In this way, he intended to convey to the readers the idea that Machiavelli's most precious legacy was precisely the myth of the redeemer.

In addition to Machiavelli's, other similar myths of redemption were circulating in nineteenth-century Europe. The correlations between the different accounts are hard to trace. In most cases, they originated separately from common biblical sources. It is fair, however, to assume that the various myths were helping each other. The same story, told and retold by different storytellers, in different voices and with a few adaptations, becomes more attractive and more persuasive. Alessandro Manzoni invoked in his ode *Marzo 1821* (*March 1821*), the same God of the Exodus that Machiavelli had invoked in his "Exhortation":

Yes, that God who enclosed in a ruby wave
the cruel who was chasing Israel
that God who put the mallet into the vigorous Giaele's
     hand
and guided the blow.

His God sides with the oppressed and wants to help them
because their cause is just:

> If the land on which you moaned oppressed
> pushes the bodies of your oppressors, who told you that
>   sterile, eternal
> will the mourning of the Italian people be?
> who told you that God, that God who heard you,
> will be deaf to our moaning?

Manzoni's God is "Father to all the peoples"; Machiavelli's is the God of the Italians. Universalistic language is
not his language. Yet, the sense of the invocation to God
is the same—that is, the promise of God's decisive help
to the people who are willing to fight for their emancipation. *Va' Pensiero*, the true hymn of Italian Risorgimento
that Verdi composed around 1842 for *Nabucco*, also powerfully appeals to a God who intervenes to help the oppressed people transform their sufferance into virtue, just
like Machiavelli's "Exhortation":

> *O t'ispiri il Signore un concento*
> Or else let the Lord inspire you with a harmony
> *Che ne infonda al patire virtù*
> Which shall instill virtue in our suffering!"

The moral message of Machiavelli's "Exhortation" could
not have been rendered in a better way.

Outside Italy, the Machiavellian myth found admirers
who finely rephrased it. In England, the most influential
proponent of the interpretation of Machiavelli as a prophet

of national emancipation was the liberal historian and politician Thomas Macaulay. In the essay he published in 1827 in the *Edinburgh Review*, later reprinted many times in his collected works, he vigorously defended Machiavelli from the charges of immorality and praised him as a man totally devoted to the cause of the liberty of his country: "It is notorious that Machiavelli was, through life, a zealous republican. In the same year in which he composed his manual of King-craft, he suffered imprisonment and torture in the cause of public liberty. It seems inconceivable that the martyr of freedom should have designedly acted as the apostle of tyranny." "We are acquainted," Macaulay insists, "with few writings which exhibit so much elevation of sentiment, so pure and warm zeal for the public good, or so just a view of the duties and rights of citizens, as those of Machiavelli."[22]

For Macaulay, Machiavelli suffered "most strongly" the humiliations and the cruelties that foreign armies repeatedly inflicted on his country ("the swinish intemperance of Switzerland, the wolfish avarice of Spain, the gross licentiousness of the French"), correctly identified the cause in Italy's political disunion and military weakness, and generously labored to provide the right remedy. The "noble and pathetic exhortation with which the *Prince* concludes," Macaulay stresses, shows how strongly the writer felt about Italy's emancipation. To this "joyless and thankless duty," Machiavelli dedicated his best energies: "In the energetic language of the prophet, he was 'made for the sight of his eyes which he saw'—disunion in the council, effeminacy in the camp, liberty extinguished, commerce decaying, national honor sullied, an enlightened and flourishing people given over to the ferocity of ignorant savages."[23]

Because of the prophetic force of his writings, Macaulay concluded, Machiavelli deserves the monument erected in his memory in Santa Croce and the reverence of all "who can distinguish the virtues of a great mind through the corruptions of a degenerate age." But Machiavelli's true triumph will be the fulfillment of his political and moral prophecy—that is, "when the foreign yoke shall be broken, when a second Proccita [sic] shall avenge the wrongs of Naples, when a happier Rienzi shall restore the good estate of Rome, when the streets of Florence and Bologna shall again resound with their ancient war cry—Popolo; popolo; muoiano i tiranni!"[24]

As movements for national emancipation gained momentum in Europe, scholars appreciated *The Prince* as a manifesto of political emancipation, and indeed as the hymn of the new revolutionary ideas. Edgar Quinet (1803–75) in his *Les Révolutions d'Italie* (*The Revolutions of Italy*), a work that had a wide circulation in the nineteenth century, stressed that the origin of Machiavelli's thought was the defeat of Savonarola, who tried to regenerate Florence and Italy with the language of the early church and preached that aid should be sought only in God, and that his listeners should arm themselves with the sword of prayer and await a miracle. Machiavelli, in contrast, attempted to revive Italy from its moral death by means of a politics carried on "without God, without providence, without religion, neither pagan, nor Christian."[25] In the face of Italy's moral depravity, Machiavelli did not raise the banner of a moral and religious reform but rather issued an appeal for a redeemer who would employ force to bring about a rebirth. His violent and impassioned theory left no room for the art of conquering the human soul with religion. Sustained by a love of the fatherland equal to that of the great men of antiquity, Machiavelli accepted neither the death of Italy nor a sense of Christian resignation. He attempted to make a heroic intellectual effort to find a cure for the ills of Italy in both political intelligence and force. In this spirit, Quinet remarks, Machiavelli put aside the mask of the cold observer of political life and composed his exhortation to liberate Italy from the barbarians—"the *Marseillaise* of the sixteenth century"—a cry of triumph in which he infused all his love of country. Before reaching the final exhortation, Machiavelli had to walk his way through an "infernal path," but that final chapter, Quinet assured us, amply absolves him.[26]

The most influential prophet of the Italian Risorgimento, Giuseppe Mazzini, was much less inclined to pardon Machiavelli's leniency toward moral and political hypocrisy. As a result, Machiavelli's classical republicanism and Mazzini's new republicanism never merged: Mazzini's theory of social and political emancipation did not benefit from Machiavelli's realism, and Machiavelli did not become the acclaimed hero of all the militants of the Italian Risorgimento.[27] Mazzini highly praised Machiavelli as the prophet of the unification of Italy who served as something like an ideal bond linking Dante and Alfieri. In his *Address to the Provisional Government in Paris, March 22, 1848*, written on behalf of the Italian Association, Mazzini eloquently placed Machiavelli among the great Italians who foresaw and preached the noble ideal of the political unification of the peninsula.[28] Nonetheless, he considered Machiavelli's idea not quite adequate to the rebirth of the fatherland:

Nations are not regenerated with lies, Machiavelli, whom
the false prophets of liberty have long imitated, profan-
ing his knowledge, lived in a time when church, principality, and foreigners had extinguished an era of Italian
life and after attempting the greatest dangers on behalf
of the fatherland and having undergone prison and torture to see if there might be some way of extracting a
spark of action, proceeded, God only knows with what
misunderstood and uncomforted pain, to undertake an
anatomy of the cadaver, to mark its scars, to enumer-
ate the princely, courtly, and priestly worms squirming
within it, and offered that spectacle to the better posterity that he foresaw, just as the Spartan fathers led their
young before the drunken Helot in order to teach them
to avoid the shame of intemperance. And we are at the
dawn of an era, stirred by the breath of a new life; and
what could we ever learn from the pages of Machiavelli
save for an understanding of the tactics of the wicked to
avoid them and disappoint them?[29]

As better teachers of moral and political emancipation
than Machiavelli, Mazzini indicated Socrates and Jesus:

No; we cannot revive through Jesuitism, we cannot regenerate a people with lies. Jesuitism is the tool of dying
religions; lies are the art of a people condemned to servitude. Socrates and Jesus both died, at the hand of an
executioner, a corporeal death, but their souls live on im-
mortally, transfused from century to century in the finer
life of ensuing generations. All moral and philosophical progress that has been achieved over the past two

thousand years hearkens back to the name of Socrates, and an entire era of emancipatory civilization drew for fourteen centuries its auspices from the sainted name of Jesus: all of Machiavelli's learning was nothing more than a funereal lamp that illuminated the tomb of the second life of Italy; and if the powerful anatomist of a period of shame and decay were to glimpse the pygmies who today busy themselves in imitating him around the cradle of the third life, he would fume with a great-hearted wrath against them.[30]

MACHIAVELLI'S *PRINCE* AND ITALY'S MORAL AND POLITICAL REFORMATION

Once the Risorgimento was over, and Italy attained its national unity and independence, liberal historians began to reexamine Machiavelli's myth of the founder. Francesco De Sanctis, for instance, a towering figure in post-Risorgimento Italy, admired Machiavelli the patriot but he attributed him with, and severely criticized, the belief that the fatherland "is a god, higher even than morality, and higher than law. God had come out of Heaven and descended to the earth [. . .]. Liberty [for Machiavelli] meant the participation, in some degree, of all the citizens in public affairs. The rights of man did not enter as yet into the code of freedom. Man was not as yet an autonomous being, an end in himself: he was the instrument of his country, or what was even worse, of the state [. . .] the individual absorbed into society, or as they called it then, 'the omnipotence of the state.' "[31] If political reform were to become a reality,

De Sanctis wrote, it needed to be accompanied by a religious reform that could recognize in an unambiguous manner the value of the individual. Yet, with these qualifications,
he praised Machiavelli as the prophet of Italian liberty:

> Developed, corrected, simplified, and in part realized,
> Machiavellism is the program of the modern world, and
> the great nations are the nations that come nearest to re-
> alizing it. Let us be proud of our Machiavelli. Whenever
> a part of the ancient building crumbles, let there be glory
> to Machiavelli, and whenever a part of the new is built,
> let there be glory to Machiavelli! Even as I am writing
> these words the bells are ringing far and wide, unceas-
> ingly, telling that the Italians are in Rome: the temporal
> power is falling, the people are shouting, "Long live the
> unity of Italy!" Let there be glory to Machiavelli![32]

Pasquale Villari (1827–1917)—one of the most respected intellectuals of late-nineteenth-century Italy—
severely criticized Machiavelli's ideas on religion and his
failure to recognize the need for a religious reform capable
of sustaining the efforts for political emancipation. In his
book *Niccolò Machiavelli e i suoi tempi* (*The Life and Times of
Niccolò Machiavelli*; 1877–82)—written with the ambition
of understanding both the vices of Italy "against which we
struggle today" and the virtues of Italy, "which helped us to
rise again"[33]—he argued that Machiavelli felt and showed
with words and actions his "ardent and irresistible love for
liberty, his country, and even for virtue," but that he had
the great shortcoming of theorizing a political redemption
without religious reform.[34]

The "Exhortation," Villari stressed, comprises "the synthesis of the *Prince* and of Machiavelli's political ideas."[35] Here the author's fundamental ideas are reduced to unity by their personification in the legislator and ruler who is to organize and regenerate the country. This ideal, this ideal personage, first inspired in Machiavelli's mind by examples of antiquity and based on the model of Romulus, Lycurgus, and Solon, is also frequently brought before us in the pages of the *Discourses*, sometimes singly and in an almost abstract form, while at other times in a more concrete and modern shape in association with Francesco Sforza, Caesar Borgia, and Ferdinand the Catholic. In *The Prince*, we have no longer the abstraction, "but the concrete, real and living personage; the type and image of the sovereign of the Renaissance."[36]

For Villari, Machiavelli did not compose the "Exhortation" to please the Medici but to force upon them his vision for Italy. It was of course a pure illusion of Machiavelli's poetic mind. Italians were too corrupt and the Medici utterly incapable of comprehending the nobility of Machiavelli's vision. Nevertheless, Villari noted,

> this creation of a thinker's brain had all the importance of an historical incident, for Machiavelli had foreseen that which was bound to ensue in Europe, and by his proclamation of it, helped to precipitate the course of events. It is beyond doubt that the *Prince* had a more direct action upon real life than any other book in the world, and a larger share in emancipating Europe from the Middle Ages.[37]

What made *The Prince* so powerful was precisely Machiavelli's ability, in the "Exhortation," to draw near the people and near society, to speak their voice, to "represent their highest aspirations, personifying their most secret conscience." Machiavelli's vision proved to be, therefore, a political prophecy of the finest kind: "All that he wrote in his exhortation appears an almost exact description of that which, after an interval of three centuries and half, we have seen accomplished under our own eyes. Only, therefore, after facts have proved the truth of the dream, was it possible to grasp the whole conception of the Florentine Secretary, and appreciate the prodigious originality of his mind."[38]

Another historian committed to keeping alive the ideals of the Risorgimento, Oreste Tommasini (1844–1919), in his monumental work *La vita e gli scritti di Niccolò Machiavelli nella loro relazione col Machiavellismo* (*The Life and Writings of Niccolò Machiavelli in Their Connection with Machiavellism*; 1883–1911), asserted even more forcefully than Villari that *The Prince*'s true message is in the "Exhortation." To bring about a *risorgimento* ("resurrection" or "rebirth") through any means possible was "among the most vibrant and personal of Machiavelli's aspirations," Tommasini remarked, even if his exhortation was not understood and had no resonance in Italy. Machiavelli was free of any theological prejudice and believed like Cromwell, Robespierre, Garibaldi, and Mazzini, that divinity was honored through works. Machiavelli saw that the true problem afflicting Italy was a bad religious education and would have liked to see in Italy the rebirth of a solid, simple, and practical religious faith founded upon a "virile charity." In *The Prince*, Tommasini stressed, Machiavelli wanted the ideal of the Italian resurgence to become the sentiment and the

faith capable of moving the people to fight, to find its martyrs, to win victories, and to achieve its logical and ineluc-
table effects, all the more vast the less imminent they may
prove to be.[39]

The first critical edition of *The Prince* that appeared in
post-Risorgimento Italy, edited by Professor Giuseppe
Lisio, also insisted that the true reason for the immortality
of Machiavelli's tract is its unsurpassed ability to describe
and illustrate the tragic figure of the founder of a state and
of a nation who is capable with outstanding individual energy to change society. That creation of the "eternal type"
("tipo eterno") of individual energy was the invention of
Machiavelli's mind, a work of genius of a man who was
able better than anyone else of understanding political reality.[40] History teaches us, Lisio stressed, that times offer
great men the opportunity of displaying their marvelous
virtue: "Who can imagine England without Cromwell,
or the United States without Washington, or revolutionary France without Napoleon I? And what would our Italy
be without Camillo Cavour, or modern Germany without
Otto von Bismarck?"[41] Those who have accused Machiavelli of being just a cold observer of political life forget that
his ideal was the redeemer. The tragic figure of *The Prince*,
Lisio concluded, governing a happy people of a free and
strong Italy still seduces us with its mysterious charm like
a mountaintop in the light of the sunset, still visible as the
night has already surrounded the rest.[42]

In spite of the efforts of Mazzini and many other leaders and militants, the Risorgimento did not produce the
much-looked-for religious and moral reformation. Fifty
years after the completion of its unification, Italy had

instead a fascist regime, with its new political religion centered on the omnipotent and redemptive Duce, the ideology transformed in a set of dogmas, new symbols, and new rituals. Predictably, fascist ideologists made repeated efforts to interpret Machiavelli as an advocate of the principle that political action is primarily a matter of force. Mussolini himself, as early as 1924, delivered the keynote speech that launched the new trend of Machiavelli as theorist of pure force. After having reassured the readers that he was not going to speak as a scholar but, more modestly, just to present "his own" Machiavelli, Mussolini built his argument on the premise that the author of *The Prince* held a deeply grim view of human beings and of Italians in particular, and since his time, things in Italy had gotten even worse. Italians do all they can to avoid taxes, to disobey the laws, to run away from military duties, and to pursue their egotistic pleasures. Liberal and democratic ideologies—with their much boasted principle of popular sovereignty—have dramatically failed to provide a solution to the contrast between the citizens and the state. What is needed to remedy the Italian problem, therefore, is not consent, but force: the force of a prince who, like Machiavelli's armed prophets, is capable of forcing them to believe. Having set things straight, Mussolini ended his speech with the assertion that "the word prince must be taken to mean state: in Machiavelli's concept the prince is the State."[43]

Other scholars followed the Duce's input and further elaborated the idea of Machiavelli as theorist of force. Achille Norsa, for instance, maintained that the single greatest merit of Machiavelli was to have discovered that "force is the law of politics" and that strength is the only logic that makes human actions intelligible in the field of politics. By *force*, he meant force of will, determination to fight, and military organization. For Norsa, it was a minor and weak point of Machiavelli to have believed for a moment in the possibility that the individual effort of a courageous and fortunate prince would have saved Italy and freed it from the barbarians.[44] In the same way, it was an understandable moment of weakness on Machiavelli's part to have been, oppressed by poverty, a flatterer. What really excited his mind was to investigate how a domineering will originates and affirms and how the personality of a leader succeeds in subordinating with his virtue the will of the majority of men.[45] This inclination inspired Machiavelli's superb design of the new prince, the terrifying and grandiose figure that dominates the whole treatise: he is the sole entity responsible for the future of his people; he is the only one who can with his will transform a multitude of dispersed men into a people, infusing in it a conscience, a soul, and modeling it in a political unity, transforming subjects into good soldiers.[46] *The Prince*, Norsa concluded, can be compared to the masterpieces of architecture produced by Alberti or Bramante. Machiavelli's sincere patriotism, his biblical style, and the prophetic warmth of the exhortation in which he invokes a magnanimous prince to redeem Italy are for Norsa issues of secondary importance, compared to the great discovery of the principle of force.

In the same years, interestingly, the best minds of the antifascist front rediscovered the myth of Machiavelli's prince as a liberator and a prophet. Against the fascist notion of Machiavelli as theorist of force, the antifascists proposed Machiavelli as prophet of liberty, the citizen who exhorted the Italians, through the myth of the new prince, to commit themselves to the arduous struggle for their political emancipation. The political theorist who opened this new interpretive path was Piero Gobetti (1901–26), a young man who felt himself intellectually and spiritually very close to the Florentine secretary. Through the books of Vittorio Alfieri, whom he had studied for his baccalaureate thesis at the University of Turin, Gobetti discovered in Machiavelli's pages a powerful religion of liberty. For him, Machiavelli was not a pure technician of politics, but a fine patriot who wrote in favor of political action even though he was well aware that no one would be able to put into practice his teachings and his exhortations in his own lifetime.

Machiavelli had placed in opposition to the God who teaches us to be servile and deprives people of the strength to achieve great things a God who lives in Christ the "creator of political liberty." Based on this God, Gobetti announced a religion of liberty that should inspire a group of citizens capable of fighting on behalf of liberty because they must, and not because they are sure of victory. It was the religion of the founders of political liberty, who attain their goal because they are capable of generating enthusiasm and devotion in their people, a religion that "is no longer a source of comfort for the weak, but of security for the strong, no longer a cult of a transcendent activity, but of our own activity, no longer faith but responsibility."[47] Gobetti recognized this religious spirit in the pages of Machiavelli: "Our Reformation," Gobetti wrote, with remarkable intellectual boldness, "was Machiavelli," an isolated individual, a political theorist, not a prince or the leader of an army.

Machiavelli's ideals failed to find a social terrain on which to establish a foundation, or men that could live by them. He was a modern man because he founded a conception of the State that rebelled against the transcendent, and conceived of an *art of politics* as the organization of the practical, as well as "professing a religiosity of practical action." In order to attain its political reform, Gobetti remarked, Italy needed this kind of civil religion or religion of liberty, the religion that Machiavelli taught us as a "citizen who is an expert in historical contingencies," not the "noisy program" of the "peasant" Luther.[48]

When Gobetti was writing these notes, Federico Chabod, soon to become one of the most renowned historians of the twentieth century, composed the introduction to a new edition of *The Prince* that appeared in 1924. In this truly groundbreaking essay, he stressed that Machiavelli's enduring political and moral lesson is in the chapter on fortune and in the "Exhortation," and that the whole essay is written in view of the final appeal to a redemptive political action:

> Observe how the digression on Fortune is almost immediately robbed of its doctrinal severity by the interpolation of a vivid simile, how it terminates in a vigorously expressive image. The abstract scheme is first thrown into confusion by the onrush of the swollen turbid river, then disappears completely in face of the almost sculptural representation of the woman who allows herself to be beaten and submits to young men. This imperceptible transition from reasoning to imagination, from the concept to the effigy, from the systematic argument to the

rapidly-drawn picture, is typical of Machiavelli, who is now dominated by his imagination and his emotions. And suddenly there comes the final exhortation, already implicit in the half logical, half imaginative analysis of Fortune, implicit for that matter in the entire treatise, from the first deduction to the last, from the most trivial comment to the boldest theorization.[49]

For Chabod, Machiavelli composed his essay to give life to the vision of new political orders apt to resurrect Italy from oppression:

And if in the end his faith and importunity can no longer be suppressed, if they vent themselves in a sudden outpouring of feeling and find their complement in that enslaved, beaten and disrupted Italy which compels pity, this is nothing but the final expression of that non-logical, non-intellective world which has been growing within the rational world and all through the work. Having put reality and the conventional interpretation of history behind him, Niccolò must return to them with that new germ of life which he has engendered by transforming his experience into creativeness and his memories—both classical and modern—into a renewed political consciousness.[50]

Machiavelli wrote to motivate action, not to gain the approbation of the learned community. That is why the first chapters of *The Prince* are written in the style of syllogisms, but the last one "with the introduction of Biblical reminiscences opens out to limitless horizons; when the writer allows his hopes to revive and lifts his eyes from his beaten and enslaved Italy, [the text] aspires to the austere emotion of a religious warning."[51] The biblical images serve the purpose of reinforcing the exhortations with the amplitude and the austerity of the divine warning.

Following Benedetto Croce, Chabod claimed that Machiavelli's "universal influence" consists, as I have mentioned, in the discovery that the foundation of new political orders demands that political action is conceived as being autonomous from ethics. He also stressed, however, that the deepest and most enduring value of *The Prince* was its powerful redemptive message, at least for the Italians:

> And there is yet another consideration, perhaps more closely bound with Italian life alone, which, as it were, isolates *The Prince* and makes us re-read it not without a vague, secret emotion. Machiavelli's re-affirmation of the importance of open resistance, which requires austerity of mind as well as an untroubled conscience; his condemnation of laziness, complacency and "style," whose counterparts are hard work, danger and ceaseless struggle; his transformation of a life that is a precise and bitter duty into faith and passion—these things betokened a profundity and an asceticism which became for Italians a lesson in life.[52]

The most impressive revision and reenactment of the Machiavellian myth of the redeemer is, however, to be found in Antonio Gramsci's prison notebooks. In his reflections on the possibility of a new beginning of the communist movement in Europe after the tragic defeats of the

1920s and early 1930s, Gramsci not only rediscovered and reworked the theme of the religious and moral reform as a necessary condition for political and social emancipation, but also rewrote the myth of the Machiavellian founder to adapt it to a theory of social emancipation to be led by a collective leadership with the active participation of large masses of men and women at last free from passivity, indifference, and resignation. Through Gramsci's revision, the myth takes a new form and reveals an impressive political and moral strength; the strength, of course, of a myth— that is, its power to generate beliefs, to excite imagination, and above all to encourage and sustain political and social action.

Gramsci began his reinterpretation by making it clear that *The Prince* is not a systematic treatise, but a "living work" ("libro vivente") in which "political ideology and political science are fused in the dramatic form of the 'myth.'" Before Machiavelli, "political science had taken the form either of the Utopia or of the scholarly treatise. Machiavelli combining the two, gave imaginative and artistic form to his conception by embodying the doctrinal, rational element in the person of a *condottiere*, who represents plastically and 'anthropomorphically' the symbol of the 'collective will.'"[53] Machiavelli's masterful design of the new prince "sets in motion the artistic imagination of the people that the writer wants to convince, and in this way he intends to excite their political passions."[54]

The intellectual and political core of *The Prince* is therefore to be identified precisely in the "Exhortation": "the 'mythical' character of the book . . . is due also to its conclusion; having described the ideal *condottiere*, Machiavelli here, in a passage of great artistic effect, invokes the real *condottiere* who is to incarnate him historically. This passionate invocation reflects back on the entire book, and is precisely what gives it its dramatic character."[55] In fact, Machiavelli has composed the entire treatise having in mind the creation of the myth of the redeemer:

> The utopian character of *The Prince* lies in the fact that the Prince had no real historical existence; he did not present himself immediately and objectively, but was a pure theoretical abstraction—a symbol of the leader and ideal *condottiere*. However, in a dramatic movement of great effect, the elements of passion and myth which occur throughout the book are drawn together and brought to life in the conclusion, in the invocation of a prince who "really exists."[56]

In the "Exhortation," Machiavelli speaks in his own voice, or, more precisely, speaks with the voice of a prophet who is capable of representing the deep and historically determined aspirations of his own people and points to them the road to emancipation by designing before their eyes the new prince and their redeemer. Gramsci's words deserve to be quoted at length because of their interpretive force and their historical relevance:

> Throughout the book, Machiavelli discusses what the Prince must be like if he is to lead a people to found a new State; the argument is developed with rigorous logic, and with detachment. In the conclusion Machiavelli merges with the people, becomes the people; not however, some

"generic" people, but the people whom he, Machiavelli,
has convinced by the preceding argument—the people
whose consciousness and whose expression he becomes
and feels himself to be, with whom he feels identified.
The entire "logical" argument now appears as nothing
other than auto reflection on the part of the people—an
inner reasoning worked out in the popular consciousness, whose conclusion is a cry of passionate urgency.
The passion, from discussion of itself, becomes once
again "emotion," fever, fanatical desire for action. This is
why the epilogue of *The Prince* is not something extrin-
sic, tacked on, rhetorical, but has to be understood as a
necessary element of the work—indeed as the element
which gives the entire work its true color, and makes it a
kind of "political manifesto."[57]

After having identified *The Prince* as a political manifesto artistically composed in view of the elaboration of a
prophetic myth, the next step of Gramsci's interpretation
was to clarify the much debated issue of whom the treatise
was written for. Machiavelli has written *The Prince*, Gramsci
briskly asserts, for everyone and for no one.[58] He did not
intend to teach the secrets of statecraft to the ruling classes
of his time, who surely did not need his wisdom. Had he
intended to do such a thing, he would have composed, like
many others did, a private memorandum or letter. Machiavelli really wanted to teach, we must then suppose, those
who do not know—that is, the "revolutionary classes of the
time, the Italian 'people' or 'nation,' the citizen democracy
which gave birth to men like Savonarola and Pier Soderini,
rather than to a Castruccio or a Valentino." The kind of

political and moral teaching that Machiavelli wanted to offer to these classes, was not merely negative—a mere hatred of tyranny and monarchy—but also positive—that is, the mature persuasion "of the necessity of having a leader who knew what he wanted and how to obtain it, and of accepting him with enthusiasm even if his actions might conflict or appear to conflict with the generalized ideology of the time—religion."[59]

The whole issue of the autonomy of politics from ethics that the interpreters of *The Prince* have so hotly debated must be discussed, Gramsci remarks, taking into account that Machiavelli was not a mere scientist of politics, but a man of action who wants to contribute to create new social and political order. Since he was not a prince himself and did not have an army under his command, Machiavelli tried to stimulate a new collective will with the only means he had available, that is "armies of words" ("eserciti di parole"). With his armies of words, Machiavelli proclaimed "in nuce," the constituent elements of an "intellectual and moral revolution" understood as a "religious question or a conception of the world." From these elements, Gramsci developed the belief that the modern prince, the Communist party, "must and cannot fail to be the originator and organizer of a reform both intellectual and moral," capable of developing "the collective national will toward the achievement of a superior form of modern civilization."[60]

A few years after Gramsci's death in 1937, in the darkest years of the Nazi occupation, Machiavelli's *Prince* became in France a manifesto of political resistance. Augustine Renaudet, of the Collège de France, revealed this tale to us in the 1956 preface to the second edition of his book

Machiavel, which came out in 1942. Renaudet was highly
critical of Machiavelli's moral views and praised him only
for his method of historical and political investigation.[61]
He also noted that Machiavelli's positive style of thinking was somehow tainted by his poetic imagination and his
propensity to create myths like that of the Duke Valentino
and, even more, that of a redeemer of Italy: "Like Dante,
like Petrarch, Machiavelli too invokes a redeemer, a Theseus, a Moses, or a Cyrus. While the government of a state
must be a republican work, the foundation, and even more
so the reform of a state, demand the action of one man
alone."[62] Yet Renaudet's book was avidly read under the
Nazi occupation, and Machiavelli, became "what he had
never been in his life: an armed prophet [*prophète armé*],
one of those who are often invoked by defeated and hu-
miliated people."[63]

Three years later, the idea of Machiavelli as a theorist
of political emancipation was taken up by the historian
of literature Luigi Russo. In his book *Machiavelli*, dedicated to two anti-Fascist martyrs, Nello Rosselli (d. 1937)
and Leone Ginzburg (d. 1944), Russo explained that Machiavelli was a creator and a poet: unable to give life to
political orders and events, he dedicated his energies to
serve an "eternal ideal." Like a true artist, Russo remarked,
Machiavelli was disinterested. For this reason, he always
inclined, in his life and his thinking, to prefer extreme, unusual, unconventional ideas over middle ground, moder-
ate, conventional positions.[64] Like Federico Chabod, Russo
stressed that he composed *The Prince* all at once, as an or-
ganic work, inspired by the ideal of a new prince capable of
unifying and liberating Italy. The "Exhortation" is therefore

the logical and necessary conclusion of *The Prince,* its ideal beginning and *telos.*

Russo read the "Exhortation" as a text written from the perspective that political redemption must be achieved from the top down, thanks to a great political leader, not the result of a moral regeneration of a whole people. Russo also stressed that Machiavelli had a quite limited, in terms of territory, vision of Italy. In fact, he speaks only of Lombardy, the Kingdom of Naples, Tuscany, Rome, and Romagna. There is no mention of Sicily, Venice, and Piedmont. Strictly speaking, therefore, Machiavelli was not a prophet of Italian unification, as a number of fascist ideologists maintained in the 1930s.

Even though he was not prepared to follow all the way the supporters of the interpretation of Machiavelli as prophet and forerunner of the Risorgimento, Russo insisted that *The Prince* had a remarkable influence on Italian cultural and political life. Men like Mazzini and Alfieri understood well that Italians could attain and preserve political liberty only by achieving, at the same time, a genuine "moral reform." The thinkers who really understood and refined Machiavelli's teaching were not the champions of political realism, but those who stressed that alongside the "'effectual reality,' there is also 'ideal reality,' alongside the earth, heaven, how things ought to be alongside how things are." The real vindication of Machiavelli's persuasion that redemptive politics demands poetic and prophetic spirit, had been, however, the Risorgimento: "when the unity of the peninsula, an abstract prophecy at the turn of the sixteenth century, became a concrete standard at the end of the eighteenth century, and in the nineteenth century this extraordinary achievement became possible only because political action became also poetic and religious agitation."[65] Machiavelli resorts to prophetic language because he knows that "without prophetic pathos, without moral renewal, without civil conscience," ideals of political emancipation remain a mere utopia, nothing more than speculations about imagined republics.

NOTES

INTRODUCTION

1. *Contrat Social*, III, 6, in Jean-Jacques Rousseau, *Œuvres Complètes*, ed. Bernard Gagnebin and Marcel Raymond, Gallimard, Paris, 1964; English translation by Donald A. Cress, introduction by Peter Gay, Indianapolis, Hackett Publishing, 1987. The following note was inserted in the 1782 edition:

> Machiavelli was a decent man and a good citizen. But, being attached to the court of the Medicis, he could not help veiling his love of liberty in the midst of his country's oppression. The choice of his detestable hero, Caesar Borgia, clearly enough shows his hidden aim; and the contradiction between the teaching of *The Prince* and that of the *Discourses on Livy* and the *History of Florence* shows that this profound political thinker has so far been studied only by superficial or corrupt readers. The Court of Rome sternly prohibited his book. I can believe it; for it is that court it most clearly portrays.

The expression "teacher of evil" comes from Leo Strauss, *Thoughts on Machiavelli*, Glencoe, IL, Free Press, 1958, p. 3.

2. The main proponent of this view has been Benedetto Croce:

> Ed è risaputo che il Machiavelli scopre la necessità e l'autonomia della politica, della politica che è di là, o piuttosto di qua, dal bene e dal male morale, che ha le sue leggi a cui è vano ribellarsi, che non si può esorcizzare e cacciare dal

mondo con l'acqua benedetta. È questo il concetto che circola in tutta l'opera sua, e che, quantunque non vi sia formulato con quella esattezza didascalica e scolastica che sovente si scambia per filosofia, e quantunque anche vi si presenti talvolta conturbato da idoli fantastici, da figure che oscillano tra la virtù politica e la scelleraggine per ambizione di potere, è da dire nondimeno concetto profondamente filosofico, e rappresenta la vera e propria fondazione di una filosofia della politica.

Benedetto Croce, *Elementi di politica* (1925), in *Etica e politica*, ed. *Giuseppe Galasso*, Milano, Adelphi, 1994, p. 292; English translation by Salvatore Castiglione, *Politics and Morals*, New York, Philosophical Library, 1945, pp. 58–60.

Following Croce, Federico Chabod has also made a similar claim:

Mentre invece cominciava a porsi, come centro della vita postuma del Machiavelli, quella che era la grande affermazione sua di pensatore, e rappresenta il vero e profondo contributo ch'egli arrecava nella storia del pensiero umano: il nettissimo riconoscimento, cioè, dell'autonomia e della necessità della politica. . . . Con ciò Machiavelli, buttando a mare la unità medievale, diveniva uno degli iniziatori dello spirito moderno.

Federico Chabod, *Del 'Principe' di Niccolò Machiavelli* (1925), in *Scritti su Machiavelli*, introduction by Corrado Vivanti, Torino, Einaudi, 1993, pp. 99–100; English translation by David Moore, *Machiavelli and the Renaissance*, introduction by A. P. d'Entrèves, London, Bowes and Bowes, 1958, pp. 115–16.

3. Italics mine. "E nelle azioni di *tutti* li uomini, e massime de' principi, dove non è iudizio a chi reclamare, si guarda al fine."

4. A noteworthy exception is Sebastian De Grazia, *Machiavelli in Hell*, Princeton, NJ, Princeton University Press, 1989.

5. Leo Strauss, "Machiavelli's Intention: *The Prince*," *American Political Science Review* 51 (1957): 13–14, 20; reissued in his *Thoughts on Machiavelli*, Glencoe, IL, The Free Press, 1958.

6. Strauss, "Machiavelli's Intention: *The Prince*," p. 21.

7. Ibid., pp. 24–25.

8. Ibid., p. 29.

9. Hans Baron, "Machiavelli: The Republican Citizen and the Author of '*The Prince*,'" *English Historical Review* 76 (1961): 242.

10. Ibid., p. 248.

11. Ibid., p. 227.

12. Hans Baron, "The *Principe* and the Puzzle of the Date of Chapter 26," *Journal of Medieval and Renaissance Studies* XXI (1991): 101–2.

13. Quentin Skinner, *The Foundations of Modern Political Thought*, Cambridge, UK, Cambridge University Press, 1978, vol. I, pp. 113–38; see also Quentin Skinner, *Machiavelli*, Oxford, UK, Oxford University Press, 1981; and Allan H. Gilbert, *Machiavelli's Prince and Its Forerunners*, Durham, NC, Duke University Press, 1938.

14. Quentin Skinner, *Visions of Politics*, vol. II, *Renaissance Virtues*, Cambridge, UK, Cambridge University Press, 2002, p. 141.

15. Francesco Petrarca, *Ad Magnificum Franciscum de Carraria Padue dominum qualis esse debeat qui rempublicam regit*; English translation Francesco Petrarca, "How a Ruler Ought to Govern His State," in *The Earthly Republic: Italian Humanists on Government and Society*, ed. Benjamin G. Kohl and Ronald G. Witt, Philadelphia, University of Pennsylvania Press, pp. 77–78.

16. Bartholomaei Platinae, *De Principe*, ed. Giacomo Ferrau, Palermo, Il Vespro, 1979, p. 14.

17. "Ut haec legens, teipsum eaque quae cum cum summa omnium laude agis recognoscas teque"; Giovanni Pontano, *De Principe*, ed. Guido M. Cappelli, Rome, Salerno, 2003, p. 75.

18. Patricii Senensis, *De Regno et Regis institutione, libri IX*, Paris [Venice], Apud Aegidium Corbinum, 1567, vol. 9, p. 28.

19. J.G.A. Pocock, *The Machiavellian Moment*, Princeton, NJ, Princeton University Press, 1975, pp. 155–56.

20. Ibid., p. 172.

21. Ibid., p. 175.

22. Ibid., p. 180.

23. Sheldon Wolin, *Politics and Vision: Continuity and Innovation in Western Political Thought, Expanded Edition*, Princeton, NJ, and Oxford, UK, Princeton University Press, 2004, p. 179.

24. Ibid., p. 184.

25. Hannah Arendt, *On Revolution*, The Viking Press, New York 1963, pp. 30–32.

26. Ibid., p. 197.

27. A large and fascinating theme that I cannot delve into is the impact of Machiavelli's ideas on the American political thought of the founding period. See, for instance, C. Bradley Thompson, "John Adams's Machiavellian Moment," *Review of Politics* 57 (1995): 389–417; Brian F. Danoff, "Lincoln, Machiavelli, and American Political Thought," *Political Studies Quarterly* 30 (2000): 290–311; Karl Walling "Was Alexander Hamilton a Machiavellian Statesman?," *Review of Politics* 57 (1995): 419–47.

28. Michael Walzer, *The Revolution of the Saints: A Study in the Origins of Radical Politics*, Cambridge, MA, Harvard University Press, 1965, p. 9.

29. Ibid., p. 17.

30. I discussed this methodological issue in the introduction to my *As if God Existed*, Princeton, NJ, Princeton University Press, 2012, pp. 9–10.

31. Niccolò Machiavelli, *Discorsi sopra la prima deca di Tito Livio*, I, 9, in Niccolò Machiavelli, *Opere*, vol. I, ed. Corrado Vivanti, Turin, Einaudi, 1997–2005, 3 volumes. Hereafter cited as *Opere*. English translation by Harvey C. Mansfield and Nathan Tarcov, Niccolò Machiavelli, *Discourses on Livy*, Chicago and London, University of Chicago Press, 1996.

32. Niccolò Machiavelli, *Discursus florentinarum rerum*, in *Opere*, I, p. 735.

33. Niccolò Machiavelli, *Discorsi*, I, 58.

34. Antonio Gramsci, *Quaderni dal carcere*, ed. Valentino Gerratana, Turin, Einaudi, 2007, vol. 3, p. 1555.

CHAPTER ONE. *THE PRINCE* AS A REDEEMER

1. I am citing from Niccolò Machiavelli, *Opere*, vol. I, ed. Corrado Vivanti, Turin, Einaudi-Gallimard, 1997; English translation by Peter Bondanella *The Prince*, introduction by Maurizio Viroli, Oxford, UK, Oxford University Press, 2005. In some cases I have chosen to cite from *The Prince*, edited and translated by Harvey C. Mansfield, Chicago, University of Chicago Press, 1985. On Machiavelli's interpretation of Moses, see Alison Brown, "Savonarola, Machiavelli and Moses: A Changing Model," in *Florence and Italy: Renaissance Studies in Honour of Nicolai Rubinstein*, ed. Peter Denley and Caroline Elam, Westfield College, University of London, 1988, pp. 57–72; John H. Geerken, "Machiavelli's Moses and Renaissance Politics," *Journal of the History of Ideas* 60 (1999): 579–95.

2. Niccolò Machiavelli to Francesco Vettori, December 10, 1513, in *Opere*, vol. II, pp. 294–97; English translation, *Machiavelli and His Friends: Their Personal Correspondence*, trans. and ed. James B. Atkinson and David Sices, DeKalb, IL: Northern Illinois University Press, 1996, pp. 262–65.

3. Hans Baron, "The *Principe* and the Puzzle of the Date of Chapter 26," *Journal of Medieval and Renaissance Studies* XXI (1991): 83–102; Sergio Bertelli and Piero Innocenti, "Introduzione," in *Bibliografia machiavellina*, ed. S. Bertelli and P. Innocenti, Verona, Valdonega, 1979, pp. xxviii–xxxvi; Mario Martelli, "Introduzione a Niccolò Machiavelli," in *Il Principe*, ed. Mario Martelli, *Edizione Nazionale delle Opere*, I.1, Roma, Salerno Editrice, 2006, pp. 9–49.

4. I agree with Gennaro Sasso and Giorgio Inglese, who believe that Machiavelli composed the "Exhortation" before early 1514. See Gennaro Sasso, "Del ventiseiesimo capitolo, della 'provvidenza' e di altre coseì," in *Machiavelli e gli antichi e altri saggi*, Milan-Naples, Ricciardo Ricciardi, 1988, pp. 277–349; and Giorgio Inglese, "*Il Principe (De Principatibus)* di Niccolò Machiavelli," in *Letteratura Italiana. Le Opere*, ed. Alberto Asor Rosa, Turin, Einaudi, 1999, vol. I, p. 891.

5. In another context, in chapter XIII ("Of auxiliary, mixed, and citizen soldiers"), Machiavelli uses the adverb *ora* in reference to the King of France military defeats in June and August 1513: "This error, followed by others, as we can *now* observe from events, is the cause of the threats to that kingdom"; Federico Chabod, "Sulla composizione de 'Il Principe,'" in *Scritti su Machiavelli*, ed. F. Chabod, Turin, Einaudi, 1993, pp. 156–66.

6. Niccolò Machiavelli, *Discursus florentinarum rerum*, in *Opere*, I, p. 744; English translation by Allan H. Gilbert, *Machiavelli: The Chief Works*, p. 114.

7. Niccolò Machiavelli, *Dell'Arte della guerra*, VII, 7.

8. Niccolò Machiavelli, *Istorie fiorentine*, IV, 1.

9. Ibid., VI, 29.

10. Ibid.

11. *Machiavelli and His Friends*, pp. 382–83.

12. *Discorsi sopra la prima deca di Tito Livio*, I, 58.

13. Machiavelli soon regretted having dedicated a work to a Medici prince. See the dedicatory letter of the *Discorsi sopra la prima deca di Tito Livio*, to Zanobi Buondelmonti and Cosimo Rucellai, in *Opere*, I, pp. 195–96.

14. It is also worth noting that, as we know from the letter to Vettori of December 10, 1513, Machiavelli discussed the *Prince* with Filippo Casavecchia. Machiavelli's choice is quite revealing because Casavecchia, in a letter of June 17, 1509, not only called Machiavelli "a greater prophet than the Hebrews or any other nation ever had," but also expressed his enthusiastic support for his ideas on military and political affairs.

15. The only exception is an implicit but easily recognizable self-promoting line in chapter XX, where Machiavelli writes: "princes, especially those that are new, have discovered more loyalty and more utility in those men who, at the beginning of their rule, were considered suspect than in those who were trusted at first."

16. Francesco Petrarca, *Ad Magnificum Franciscum de Carraria Padue dominum qualis esse debeat qui rempublicam regit*; English translation Francesco Petrarca, "How a Ruler Ought to Govern His State," in *The Earthly Republic: Italian Humanists on Government and Society*, ed. Benjamin G. Kohl and Ronald G. Witt, Philadelphia, University of Pennsylvania Press, p. 45.

17. Ibid., p. 50.

18. Giovanni Pontano, *Ad Alphonsum Calabriae Ducem De Principe Liber* (1468), ed. Guido M. Cappelli, Rome, Salerno, 2003, pp. 16 and 24, 21 and 27.

19. Ibid., p. 37.

20. Ibid., p. 42.

21. "Ut, haec legens, teipsum eaque quae cum summa omnium laude agis recognoscas," ibid., p. 81.

22. Bartholomeus Platina, *De principe*, pp. 56–61.
23. "Tu itaque bonorum exemplo patriam tuam opibus, dignitate, auctoritate quoad fiery potest, auge et confirma," ibid., p. 66.
24. Ibid., p. 75.
25. Niccolò Machiavelli, *Il Principe*, XVII (ed. Mansfield).
26. Niccolò Machiavelli, *Discorsi sopra la prima deca di Tito Livio*, III, 28.
27. Niccolò Machiavelli, *Istorie fiorentine*, IV, 27; see also John M. Najemy, "Machiavelli and the Medici: The Lessons of Florentine Histories," *Renaissance Quarterly* 35 (1982): 551–76.
28. Niccolò Machiavelli, *Istorie fiorentine*, VII, 6.
29. Niccolò Machiavelli, *Il Principe*, VIII.
30. Niccolò Machiavelli, *Discorsi sopra la prima deca di Tito Livio*, I, 2. In its purest form, greatness of spirit was one of the most remarkable qualities of Roman citizens:

> Here two notable things are to be observed: one, how they were content to remain in such poverty, and that it was enough for those citizens to obtain honors from war, and to leave all the useful things to the public; for if they thought of enriching themselves from the war, they would have given little concern to their fields being spoiled. The other is to consider the generosity of spirit of those citizens who, when placed in charge of an army, rose above every Prince through the greatness of their souls; they not esteeming Kings or Republics, nor did anything dismay or frighten them, and afterwards when they returned to private life, they became frugal, humble, carers of their small facilities, obedient to the Magistrates, reverent to their elders, so that it appears almost impossible that the same mind should be able to bear such changes.

Discorsi sopra la prima deca di Tito Livio, III, 25.
31. Niccolò Machiavelli, *Discursus florentinarum rerum*, in *Opere*, I, p. 744.

32. For a fine review of the diffferent positions and a detailed bibliography on the subject, see Paul Larivaille, "Il capitolo IX del Principe e la crisi del 'principato civile,'" in *Cultura e scrittura di Machiavelli*, Atti del Covegno di Firenze-Pisa, October 27–30, 1997, p. 221.

33. *Discorso di Lodovico Alamanni sopra il fermare lo stato di Firenze nella devozione de' Medici*, in Rudolf von Albertini, *Firenze dalla repubblica al principato. Storia e coscienza politica*, Turin, Einaudi, 1970, pp. 376–84; and *Ricordi di Paolo Vettori al cardinale de' Medici sopra le cose di Firenze*, in ibid., pp. 357–59.

34. See for instance Goro Gheri, *Istruzione per Roma*, in Rudolf von Albertini, *Firenze dalla repubblica al principato* pp. 360–64.

35. Niccolò Machiavelli to Francesco Vettori, January 31, 1515, in *Opere*, vol. II, pp. 349–51; English translation, *Machiavelli and His Friends*, pp. 312–13.

36. Niccolò Machiavelli, *Il Principe*, IX.

37. Ibid., XXIV.

38. Ibid., XX.

39. Ibid., IX.

40. Ibid., IX.

41. Niccolò Machiavelli to Francesco Guicciardini, May 17, 1521, in *Opere*, II, p. 372; English translation, *Machiavelli and His Friends*, p. 336. Machiavelli expresses his love of the fatherland also in the opening of his *A Dialogue on Language* (*Dialogo intorno alla nostra lingua*), in *Opere*, III, p. 261:

> Whenever I have had an opportunity of honouring my country, even if this involved me in trouble and danger, I have done it willingly, for a man is under no greater obligation than to his country; he owes his very existence, and later, all the benefits that nature, and fortune offer him, to her. And the nobler one's country, the greater one's obligation. In

fact he who shows himself by thought and deed an enemy of his country deserves the name of parricide, even if he has a legitimate grievance.

English translation, *The Literary Works of Machiavelli: With Selections from the Private Correspondence*, ed. and trans. J. R. Hale, London and New York, Oxford University Press, 1961, p. 175.

42. Niccolò Machiavelli to Francesco Vettori, December 10, 1513, in *Opere*, II, p. 297.

43. Piero Soderini to Niccolò Machiavelli, April 13, 1521, in *Opere*, II, pp. 369–70.

44. As he stated in the *Discorsi sopra la prima deca di Tito Livio*, III, 47, "a good citizen ought to forget private injuries for love of his fatherland." See also Machiavelli's portrait of Francesco Valori as a citizen dedicated to the good of his fatherland in *Opere*, III, pp. 255–56.

45. Niccolò Machiavelli to Giovanni Vernacci, June 26, 1513, in *Opere*, II, p. 264; English translation, *Machiavelli and His Friends*, p. 239.

46. Niccolò Machiavelli to Giovanni Vernacci, August 4, 1513, in *Opere*, II, p. 271; English translation, *Machiavelli and His Friends*, p. 244.

47. Niccolò Machiavelli to Francesco Vettori, June 10, 1514, in *Opere*, II, pp. 325–60; English translation, *Machiavelli and His Friends*, p. 290.

48. Niccolò Machiavelli to Francesco Vettori, August 3, 1514, in *Opere*, II, pp. 328–29; English translation, *Machiavelli and His Friends*, pp. 292–93.

49. Niccolò Machiavelli to Francesco Vettori, January 31, 1515, in *Opere*, II, p. 351; English translation, *Machiavelli and His Friends*, p. 314.

50. Niccolò Machiavelli to Giovanni Vernacci, August 18, 1515, in *Opere*, II, p. 349; English translation, *Machiavelli and His Friends*, p. 314.

51. Niccolò Machiavelli to Giovanni Vernacci, November 19, 1515, in *Opere*, II, p. 352; English translation, *Machiavelli and His Friends*, p. 314.

52. Niccolò Machiavelli to Giovanni Vernacci, February 15, 1516, in *Opere*, II, p. 353; English translation, *Machiavelli and His Friends*, p. 315.

53. Niccolò Machiavelli to Giovanni Vernacci, June 8, 1517, in *Opere*, II, p. 354; English translation, *Machiavelli and His Friends*, p. 316.

54. Niccolò Machiavelli to Giovanni Vernacci, January 5 and January 25, 1518, in *Opere*, II, pp. 357–59; English translation, *Machiavelli and His Friends*, p. 319.

55. See also Federico Chabod, *Sulla composizione de "Il Principe" di Niccolò Machiavelli* (1927), in Chabod, *Scritti su Machiavelli*, p. 158.

56. Niccolò Machiavelli to Francesco Vettori, August 10, 1513, in *Opere*, II, pp. 277–78; English translation, *Machiavelli and His Friends*, pp. 249–50.

57. Niccolò Machiavelli to Francesco Vettori, December 10, 1513, in *Opere*, II, p. 297; English translation, *Machiavelli and His Friends*, p. 265.

58. Francesco Vettori wrote to Machiavelli: "Examine everything, and I know you have such intelligence that although two years have gone by since you have left the shop, I do not think you have forgotten the art." Francesco Vettori to Niccolò Machiavelli, December 3, 1514, in *Opere*, II, p. 330; English translation, *Machiavelli and His Friends*, p. 294.

CHAPTER TWO. A REALIST WITH IMAGINATION

1. Niccolò Machiavelli to Francesco Vettori, January 31, 1515, in *Opere*, II, p. 349; English translation, *Machiavelli and His Friends*, p. 312.

2. Niccolò Machiavelli to Francesco Vettori, April 9, 1513 in *Opere*, II, p. 241; English translation, *Machiavelli and His Friends*, p. 225.
3. Niccolò Machiavelli to Ludovico Alamanni, December 17, 1517, in *Opere*, II, p. 357; English translation, *Machiavelli and His Friends*, p. 318.
4. See Gennaro Sasso, *Il "celebrato sogno" di Machiavelli*, in *Machiavelli e gli antichi e altri saggi*, Milan-Naples, Ricciardi, 1988, vol. III, pp. 211–94; and *Paralipomeni al "sogno" di Machiavelli*, ibid., vol. IV, pp. 325–60.
5. I have discussed this issue at length in my *From Politics to Reason of State: The Acquisition and Transformation of the Language of Politics*, Cambridge, UK, Cambridge University Press, 1992, pp. 178–80.
6. See Niccolò Machiavelli to Francesco Guicciardini, March 15, 1526, in *Opere*, II, pp. 418–22; English translation, *Machiavelli and His Friends*, pp. 380–83.
7. Roberto Ridolfi, *Vita di Niccolò Machiavelli*, 7th ed., Florence, Sansoni, 1978; English translation by Cecil Grayson, *The Life of Niccolò Machiavelli*, London: Routledge and Kegan Paul, 1963.
8. Guicciardini wrote: "Tucta la Corte romana, tucta la cristiana gregge, cominciando a parerli vedere quelle che lunghissimo tempo ha desiderato ma non mai sino a hora sperato, si accinge colli animi et si ordina a seguitare sì gloriose sì sancte insegne a una impresa piena di tanto giusta vendecta, piena di tanta pietà, piena di tanta religione." God, Guicciardini continued, has conferred the kingdom upon Francis I, and the papacy upon Leo X for no other purpose than the liberation of Jerusalem. As the following lines indicate, the similarity with Machiavelli's language is impressive: "Hoggi ha la Chiesa recuperato el braccio suo, hoggi tucta integra et unita

si può con tucte le forze volgere a opere degne della Chiesa, degne di uno sommo Pontefice; la materia è disposta, non manca altro che introdurvi la forma." See Roberto Ridolfi, *Vita di Francesco Guicciardini*, Rome, Angelo Belardetti Editore, 1960, pp. 449–50.

9. Niccolò Machiavelli, *Il Principe*, XXVI.
10. Niccolò Machiavelli, *Discorsi sopra la prima deca di Tito Livio*, III, 6.
11. Tacitus, *Annals*, XV, 57, 1–2. A Latin translation of Plutarch's text, by Alamanno Rinuccini, was published in Venice in 1500 by the house of Bernardinus Venetus de Vitalibus, with the title *De claris mulieribus*.
12. Niccolò Machiavelli, *Legazioni e commissarie*, in *Opere*, II, p. 627.
13. Ibid., p. 774.
14. Niccolò Machiavelli, *Il Principe*, VII.
15. Niccolò Machiavelli, *Il Principe*, XVIII. In the *Discorsi sopra la prima deca di Tito Livio*, when he analyzes the Gracchi's struggle to introduce agrarian laws, Machiavelli stresses that their efforts provoked harsh resentment within the Roman nobility and ultimately the collapse of republican liberty. Even if their intentions were laudable, therefore, their actions cannot be praised and their example must not be followed. Like every serious realist, Machiavelli knew very well that political leaders all too frequently make lethal mistakes based on inadequate knowledge of political passions and history. The most wise Cicero, for instance, made the error of sending Octavian, the nephew of Caesar, against Mark Antony, hoping that his soldiers would have deserted him to Caesar's successor. Marcus Antonius, on the other hand, made an alliance with Octavian that led to the complete isolation of Cicero and the Senate. "That was easy to conjecture,"

Machiavelli remarks, "Cicero should have known better that from Caesar's successors or followers nothing in favor of liberty could have come." *Discorsi sopra la prima deca di Tito Livio*, I, 52.

16. Niccolò Machiavelli, *Il Principe*, III.
17. Niccolò Machiavelli, *Il Principe*, XXI. In the *Discorsi sopra la prima deca di Tito Livio*, he criticizes the policy of postponing decisions for fear of being too rash and too bold. Indecisiveness, he explains, is a typical sign of weakness: "Irresolute republics never take up good policies unless by force, because their weakness never allows them to decide where there is any doubt; and if that doubt is not suppressed by violence that drives them on, they always remain in suspense." *Discorsi sopra la prima deca di Tito Livio*, I, 38.
18. Niccolò Machiavelli to Francesco Guicciardini, in *Opere*, II, p. 621.
19. Niccolò Machiavelli to Giovan Battista Soderini, September 13–21, 1506, in *Opere*, II, pp. 135–38.
20. *Il Principe*, ch. XII; English translation, pp. 42–43. In the introduction of the *Arte della guerra*, he carries the argument further, stressing that contrary to the conventional view, which holds that military and civil life are incompatible with one another, the classics rightly teach us that the two are compatible and in fact one requires the other:

> Because all the arts that are provided for in a civil community for the sake of the common good of men, all the statutes made in it so that men will live in fear of the laws and of God, would be vain if for them there were not provided defenses, which when well ordered, preserve them, even though they themselves are not well ordered. And so, on the contrary, good customs, without military support, suffer the

same sort of injury as do the rooms of a splendid and kingly palace, even though ornamented with gems and gold, when, not being roofed over, they have nothing to protect them from the rain.

21. Niccolò Machiavelli, *Il Principe*, VI.
22. See Piero Pieri's still very useful work, *Il Rinascimento e la crisi militare italiana*, Turin, Einaudi 1952, pp. 485–535.
23. Niccolò Machiavelli, *Il Principe*, XIV.
24. In *Arte della guerra*, Machiavelli writes:

> Also very powerful in keeping the ancient soldiers well disposed were religion and the oath sworn when they were taken into service, because in all their transgressions they were threatened not alone with the ills they could fear from men but with those they could expect from God. This condition, mingled with other religious customs, many times made every sort of undertaking easy for the ancient generals, and always will make them so, where religion is feared and observed.

In Italy, by contrast, where men have no religion, and are "corrupt" and "unaccustomed to any honorable obedience," the oath taken by soldiers is of no value, and it is therefore impossible to establish a good army. In the words that Machiavelli places in the mouth of Fabrizio Colonna in *Arte della guerra*, we can perceive all the despair of a man who, drawing near to the end of his life, understands how much harm was done to Italy by the wicked religion that stripped that oath of all value: "By what God or by what saints can I have them take oath? By those they worship or those they blaspheme? What one they worship I do not know, but I know well that they blaspheme them all. How can I believe they will observe their promises to those for whom every hour they show contempt? How can those who feel contempt for God respect men?" Niccolò Machiavelli, *Dell'Arte della guerra*, VII, 7.

25. Niccolò Machiavelli, *Provisione della ordinanza*, in *Opere*, I, p. 39.
26. The idea of Machiavelli as the founder of the doctrine of reason of state has been sustained, among others, by B. Croce, *Elementi di politica*, Bari, Laterza, 1925; Friederich Meinecke, *Die Idee der Staaträson in der neurenen Geschichte*, 3rd ed., Munich and Berlin, R. Oldenbourg, 1929; J. H. Hexter, *The Vision of Politics on the Eve of the Reformation: More, Machiavelli, and Seyssel*, New York and London, Basic Books, 1973; G. Ritter, *Die Dämonie der Macht*, 6th ed., Munich, Leibniz, 1948.
27. Niccolò Machiavelli, *Arte della guerra*, IV, 4.
28. Ibid.
29. John M. Najemy on the contrary maintains that Machiavelli "is uncompromising in his insistence that imagination and truth can indeed be differentiated, and that he will speak on the basis of truth alone." The assessment of the intelligibility of political action is one of the main divergences between Machiavelli and Vettori:

> For Vettori, a rational, coherent interpretation of politics that corresponds to the essence or truth of things is not only difficult and inevitably a matter of imagination and *fantasia*; it is also "impossible," or nearly so, to translate such constructions into action, to use them to *influence* or shape events. Machiavelli's "verità effettuale" and his determination to write "cosa utile a chi la intende" are his answer to such pessimism.

Between Friends: Discourse of Power and Desire in the Machiavelli-Vettori Letters of 1513–1515, Princeton, NJ, Princeton

University Press, pp. 188 and 191, but see also pp. 58–71 and 185–201.

30. A genuine political realist like Gaetano Mosca was not prepared to list Machiavelli among his intellectual mentors. See *Elementi di scienza politica* (1896), in *Scritti politici*, ed. Giorgio Sola, Turin, UTET, 1982, pp. 780–81.

31. As a title of praise, his name has been associated with that of his compatriot Galileo: "What Galileo gave in his *Dialogues*, and what Machiavelli gave in his *Prince*," wrote Ernst Cassirer, "were really 'new sciences.' Just as Galileo's *Dynamics* became the foundation of our modern science of nature, so Machiavelli paved a new way to political science." Through his method based on empirical observations and rigorous mathematical calculations, Galileo identified the laws that govern the natural world; through empirical observations and rigorous generalizations, Machiavelli identified the laws of politics. Ernst Cassirer, *The Myth of the State*, New Haven, CT, Yale University Press, 1946, p. 130. See also Luigi Russo, *Machiavelli*, Bari, Laterza, 1949, esp. p. 71: "e si inaugura il ragionamento a catena, che sarà poi quello di Galilei e di tutta la prosa scientifica moderna. Iddio è disceso dai cieli, e anche l'arte ha scorciato le sue vie"; Leonardo Olschki, *Machiavelli the Scientist*, Berkeley, CA, Gillick Press, 1945; Augustin Renaudet, *Machiavel*, Paris, 1955; Giuseppe Prezzolini, *Machiavelli anticristo*, Rome, G. Casini, 1954; Herbert Butterfield, *The Statecraft of Machiavelli*, London, G. Bell, 1940, p. 62.

32. Niccolò Machiavelli, *Discorsi sopra la prima deca di Tito Livio*, III, 43.

33. Francesco Guicciardini, *Ricordi*, in *Opere di Francesco Guicciardini*, ed. Emanuella Lugnani Scarano, Turin, UTET, 1974, vol. I, p. 762.

34. "Io credo che come la natura ha fatto a l'uomo diverso volto, cosí li abbi fatto diverso ingegno e diversa fantasia.

Da questo nasce che ciascuno secondo lo ingegno e fantasia sua si governa"; Niccolò Machiavelli to Giovan Battista
Soderini, September 13–21, 1506, in *Opere*, II, p. 137; English translation, *Machiavelli and His Friends*, p. 135.
35. Niccolò Machiavelli, *Il Principe*, XVIII.
36. Niccolò Machiavelli, *Legazioni e commissarie*, in *Opere*, II,
    p. 774.
37. Ibid., p. 774.
38. Niccolò Machiavelli, *Discorso sopra le cose della Magna e sopra
    l'imperatore*, in *Opere*, I, p. 78.
39. Niccolò Machiavelli, *Il Principe*, XVIII.
40. Ibid.
41. Niccolò Machiavelli, *Il Principe*, XVIII.
42. Giovanni Bardazzi, "Tecniche narrative nel Machiavelli
    scrittore di lettere," in *Annali della Scuola Normale Superiore
    di Pisa*, series III, 1975, vol. V, pp. 1486–87.
43. Niccolò Machiavelli to Francesco Vettori, April 29, 1513,
    in *Opere*, II, p. 250; English translation, *Machiavelli and His
    Friends*, p. 233.
44. Francesco Vettori to Niccolò Machiavelli, March 30, 1513,
    in *Opere*, II, p. 239.
45. Niccolò Machiavelli, *Il Principe*, XXI.
46. Niccolò Machiavelli to Francesco Vettori, April 29, 1513, in
    Opere, II, p. 253.
47. Niccolò Machiavelli, *Il Principe*, XVIII.

Chapter Three. A Great Oration

1. Bernardo Machiavelli, *Libro di ricordi*, ed. Cesare Olschki,
   Florence, Le Monnier, 1954, p. 123.
2. Niccolò Machiavelli, *Legazioni e commissarie*, in *Opere*, II, pp.
   470–71.
3. Ibid., pp. 510–13.

4. Niccolò Machiavelli, *Legazioni e commissarie*, in *Opere*, II, pp. 522–23.

5. Concerning Marcello Virgilio Adriani, see Peter Godman, *From Poliziano to Machiavelli: Florentine Humanism in the High Renaissance*, Princeton, NJ, Princeton University Press, 1998; and Alison Brown, *The Return of Lucretius to Renaissance Florence*, Cambridge, MA, and London, Harvard University Press, 2010, pp. 42–67.

6. "I Dieci a Machiavelli," in *Legazioni e commissarie*, in *Opere*, II, pp. 947–48.

7. Niccolò Machiavelli, *Parole da dirle sopra la provisione del danaio, facto un poco di proemio et di scusa*, in *Opere*, I, pp. 13–16; English translation by Allan Gilbert, *Machiavelli: The Chief Works, and Others*, pp. 1440–43. On Machiavelli's early political writings, see Jean-Jacques Marchand, *Niccolò Machiavelli: i primi scritti politici (1499–1512): nascita di un pensiero e di uno stile*, Padova, Antenore, 1975.

8. "Tota autem oratio simplex et gravis et sententiis debet ornatior esse quam verbis"; Cicero, *De partitione oratoriae*, XXVII, 97, "Ita cum verba rebus aptentur, ipso materiae nitore clarescunt"; Quintilian, *Institutio oratoria*, III, VIII, 60–65. The best studies of the rhetorical composition of *The Prince* are those by John F. Tinkler, "Praise and Advice: Rhetorical Approaches in More's 'Utopia' and Machiavelli's 'Prince,'" *Sixteenth Century Journal* XIX (1988): 187–207; and Virginia Cox, "Machiavelli and the 'Rhetorica ad Herennium': Deliberative Rhetoric in 'The Prince,'" *Sixteenth Century Journal* XXVIII (1997): 1109–41. See also John F. Tinkler, "Renaissance Humanism and the Genera Eloquentiae," *Rhetorica* V (1987): 278–309; John W. O'Malley, *Praise and Blame in Renaissance Rome: Rhetoric, Doctrine, and Reform of the Sacred Orators of the Papal Court, c. 1450–1421*, Durham, NC, Duke University Press, 1979, esp. pp. 36–51;

and Victoria Kahn, *Machiavellian Rhetoric from the Counter Reformation to Milton*, Princeton, NJ, Princeton University Press, 1994, esp. pp. 18–43.

9. Niccolò Machiavelli, *Il Principe*, in *Opere*, I, pp. 117–18.

10. Niccolò Machiavelli, *Il Principe*, VI.

11. Concerning the use of examples, see Barbara Spackman, "Machiavelli and Maxims," *Yale French Studies* 77 (1990): 152; John D. Lyons, *Exemplum: The Rhetoric of Example in Early Modern France and Italy*, Princeton, NJ, Princeton University Press, 1989, esp. pp. 35–36, 49, and 63–65. See also Quentin Skinner, *Reason and Rhetoric in the Philosophy of Hobbes*, Cambridge, UK, Cambridge University Press, 1996, pp. 49–51.

12. Niccolò Machiavelli, *Il Principe*, XVIII.

13. Niccolò Machiavelli, *Il Principe*, XIII.

14. Niccolò Machiavelli, *Discorsi sopra la prima deca di Tito Livio*, III, 30. That the Bible should be read allegorically was taught by Savonarola in his sermons. See Pasquale Villari, *La storia di Girolamo Savonarola e de' suoi tempi*, 2nd ed., 2 vols., Florence, Le Monnier, 1887–88, vol. I, p. 123.

15. Niccolò Machiavelli, *Discorsi sopra la prima deca di Tito Livio*, preface.

16. Ibid.

17. Niccolò Machiavelli, *Il Principe*, XI.

18. See, for instance, what Machiavelli seriously states, in *Parole da dirle sopra la provisione del danaio, facto un poco di proemio et di scusa* (*Words to Be Spoken on the Law for Appropriating Money, after Giving a Little Introduction and Excuse*), in *Opere*, I, p. 13, and in *Discorsi*, I, 27.

19. Niccolò Machiavelli, *Il Principe*, II.

20. "Utilitas in duas partes in civili consultatione dividitur: tutam, honestam"; *Rhetorica ad Herennium*, III, II, 3.

21. *Rhetorica ad Herennium*, III, II, 3, and III, IV, 7.

22. Niccolò Machiavelli, *Il Principe*, XV.
23. "Utilitas in duas partes in civili consultatione dividitur: tutam, honestam"; *Rhetorica ad Herennium*, III, II, 3.
24. The main reason to doubt that Machiavelli intended to submit to a radical critique Quattrocento advice-books for princes is that those texts were not likely to have been available to him. Even if he had the opportunity to read them, it is quite improbable that he would have found them worthy of his study. Francesco Patrizi's *De Regno et Regis Institutione* (*Of the Kingdom and the Education of the King*), for instance, was printed for the first time in Paris in 1519, too late to be available when Machiavelli composed *The Prince*. Patrizi's work, moreover, belongs to the intellectual and political context of the court of the Aragon in Naples, which made it almost impossible for Machiavelli to have had the chance to read a copy of the manuscript. Also Diomede Carafa's book *The Office of the Good Prince*, written for Ferdinand of Naples in the 1480s, belongs to the Neapolitan context, even if Machiavelli could have consulted the Latin version of the work edited by Battista Guarino for the Duchess of Ferrara, Leonora of Aragon. Giovanni Pontano's *De Principe* (1468), published in Naples in 1490, appears to have had influence only on the political literature of the Kingdom of Naples. Machiavelli, moreover, shows little interest for the ideas of Pontano. In a letter of January 1514, Francesco Vettori mentions Machiavelli Pontano's dialogue on Fortune (*De Fortuna*) published in Naples in 1512. Machiavelli, as is well-known, was deeply interested in the theme of Fortune and her role in political affairs and in men's lives in general. Yet he had not read Pontano's work nor did he show any desire to do so.
25. See *Consulte e pratiche 1505–1512*, ed. Denis Fachard, Geneva, Droz, 1988, pp. 320–25. The importance of the *pratiche*

and the debates in the councils for an understanding of
the rhetoric of *The Prince* has been clearly emphasized by
Cox, "Machiavelli and the 'Rhetorica ad Herennium,'" esp.
p. 1136.

26. *Consulte e pratiche*, p. 353.
27. Matteo Palmieri, *Della vita civile*, ed. Felice Battaglia, Bolo-
    gna, Zanichelli, 1944, pp. 127–28.
28. Even if the orator must not propose abandoning virtue, we
    read in the *Ad Herennium*, he can state that in given cir-
    cumstances virtue does not take the form of those actions
    that we normally consider virtuous, and he can describe the
    action that he is recommending in a different way. He may
    affirm that the actions that others consider courageous are
    actually cowardly, or that actions that seem useful are in real-
    ity useless or damaging. See *Rhetorica ad Herennium*, III, III,
    6, but see also Quintilian, *Institutio Oratoria*, III.VIII. 31-
    32. Concerning the techniques of redescription, see Skinner,
    Reason and Rhetoric in the Philosophy of Hobbes, pp. 138–80.
29. According to John F. Tinkler, every serious political debate
    that aims at ultimately recommending political action must
    be practical and therefore have an intended interest, as is
    taught in both the *Rhetorica ad Herennium* and the *De in-
    ventione*, the two most important texts on rhetoric during
    the Middle Ages and the Renaissance; Tinkler, "Praise and
    Advice," p. 198. In Skinner's view, Machiavelli supports the
    "subversive suggestion" that "the question of what is *utile* in
    such matters of statecraft may have no connection with what
    is *onesto* at all"; Skinner, *Reason and Rhetoric in the Philosophy
    of Hobbes*, p. 44. Virginia Cox, who rightly points out the im-
    portance of the *Rhetorica ad Herennium* to an understanding
    of the structure of *The Prince*, claims however that Machia-
    velli wanted to demonstrate that the advantages of security
    vastly outweigh the advantages of a good reputation and,

indeed, "that the pursuit of security may in fact be the best way in the long run to ensure a lasting good repute"; Cox, "Machiavelli and the 'Rhetorica Ad Herennium,'" p. 1128.

30. Machiavelli sets forth the principle that honesty should be put second to security also in *Discorsi sopra la prima deca di Tito Livio*: "Where one deliberates entirely on the safety of his fatherland, there ought not to enter any consideration of either just or unjust, merciful or cruel, praiseworthy or ignominious; indeed every other concern put aside, one ought to follow entirely the policy that saves its life and maintains its liberty"; Machiavelli, *Discorsi sopra la prima deca di Tito Livio*, III, 41.

31. Niccolò Machiavelli, *Il Principe*, XXV. The impetus to persuade a possible redeemer that the liberation of Italy is possible moves Machiavelli to reconsider his earlier beliefs on the overwhelming power of Fortune on political affairs and human events in general; see Niccolò Machiavelli to Giovan Battista Soderini, September 13–21, 1506, in *Opere*, II, pp. 135–38; English translation, *Machiavelli and His Friends*, pp. 134–36.

32. On the "Exhortation," see Hugo Jaeckel, "What Is Machiavelli Exhorting in his 'Exhortatio'? The Extraordinaries," in *Niccolò Machiavelli politico storico letterato*, ed. Jean-Jacques Marchand, Rome, Salerno Editrice, 1996, pp. 59–84.

33. Concerning the peroration as an instrument to calm or excite passions, see Skinner, *Reason and Rhetoric in the Philosophy of Hobbes*, p. 121.

34. Cicero, *De inventione*, I, LII, 102.

35. Ibid., I, LV, 109.

36. Niccolò Machiavelli, *Istorie Fiorentine*, VI, 29.

37. Niccolò Machiavelli, *Degli spiriti beati*, in *Opere*, III, p. 28; English translation by Joseph Tusiani, *Lust and Liberty: The Poems of Machiavelli*, New York, Ivan Obolensky, 1963, p. 8.

38. Niccolò Machiavelli, *Discorsi sopra la prima deca di Tito Livio*, III, 1.

39. Niccolò Machiavelli, *Dell' Arte della guerra*, VII, 7.

CHAPTER FOUR. A PROPHET OF EMANCIPATION

1. Giuliano Procacci, *Machiavelli nella cultura europea dell'età moderna*, Rome, Bari, 1995.

2. Paul Larivaille, ed., *Une Réecriture du "Prince" de Machiavel: "De Regnandi Peritia" de Nifo*, bilingual edition, Nanterre, Publidix, 1987, p. 37.

3. Procacci, *Machiavelli nella cultura europea dell'età moderna*, pp. 74–81.

4. Albericus Gentili, *De Legationibus*, London, Thomas Vautrollarius, 1585, III, 9. See also Diego Panizza, "Machiavelli e Alberico Gentili," *Il Pensiero Politico*, II (1969): 476–83.

5. Felix Raab, *The English Face of Machiavelli: A Changing Interpretation 1500–1700*, London, Routledge & Kegan Paul, 1964, pp. 130–54.

6. Joseph Anthony Mazzeo, "Cromwell as a Machiavellian Prince in Marvell's *An Horatian Ode*," in J. A. Mazzeo, *Renaissance and Seventeenth Century Studies*, New York, Columbia University Press, and London, Routledge & Kegan Paul, 1964, pp. 166–82.

7. James Harrington, *The Commonwealth of Oceana*, in *The Political Works of James Harrington*, ed. J.G.A. Pocock, Cambridge, UK, Cambridge University Press, 1977, pp. 392–93.

8. Ibid.

9. Ibid., pp. 206–7.

10. See Tullio Gregory, *Theophrastus redivivus. Erudizione e ateismo nel Seicento*, Naples, Morano, 1979, p. 201.

11. Silvia Berti, ed., *Trattato dei tre impostori. La vita e lo spirito del Signor Benedetto de Spinoza* (*Traité des trois imposteurs* or

Treatise of the Three Impostors: The Life and Spirit of Master Benedict Benedetto de Spinosa), Turin, Einaudi, 1994, chap. XVII.

12. Giulio Cesare Vanini, *Dei mirabili arcani della natura regina e dea dei mortali*, in *Le opere di Giulio Cesare Vanini tradotte per la prima volta in italiano*, ed. Eduardo Bortone, Lecce, 1919, vol. II, pp. 327–28. See also Giorgio Spini, *Ricerca dei libertini. La teoria dell'impostura delle religioni nel Seicento italiano*, Rome, Universale di Roma, 1950.

13. Jean-Jacques Rousseau, *Du Contrat Social*, II, 9; English translation, *Rousseau's Basic Political Writings*, trans. and ed. Donald A. Cress, introduction by Peter Gay, Indianapolis: Hackett Publishing, 1987, vol. II, chap. 9.

14. Rousseau's reference to Moses is evident in the following lines:

> This sublime reason, far above the range of the common herd, is that whose decisions the legislator puts into the mouth of the immortals, in order to constrain by divine authority those whom human prudence could not move. But it is not anybody who can make the gods speak, or get himself believed when he proclaims himself their interpreter. The great soul of the legislator is the only miracle that can prove his mission. Any man may grave tablets of stone, or buy an oracle, or feign secret intercourse with some divinity, or train a bird to whisper in his ear, or find other vulgar ways of imposing on the people. He whose knowledge goes no further may perhaps gather round him a band of fools; but he will never found an empire, and his extravagances will quickly perish with him. Idle tricks form a passing tie; only wisdom can make it lasting. The Judaic law, which still subsists, and that of the child of Ishmael, which, for ten centuries, has ruled half the world, still proclaim the great men who laid them down; and, while

the pride of philosophy or the blind spirit of faction sees in them no more than lucky impostures, the true political theorist admires, in the institutions they set up, the great and powerful genius which presides over things made to endure.

Ibid.

15. Vittorio Alfieri, *Del principe e delle lettere*, ed. Luigi Russo, Florence, Le Monnier 1943; English translation by Beatrice Corrigan and Julius A. Molinaro, *The Prince and Letters*, Toronto, University of Toronto Press, 1972, p. 152.

16. Georg Wilhelm Friedrich Hegel, *The Constitution of Germany*, in *Hegel Political Writings*, Cambridge, UK, Cambridge University Press, 1999, p. 6.

17. Ibid., p. 79.

18. Ibid., p. 80.

19. Ibid., p. 82.

20. Ibid., p. 101.

21. J. G. Fichte, *Ueber Machiavelli als Schriftsteller, und Stellen aus seinen Schriften*, in J. G. Fichte, *Sämmtliche Werke*, Leipzig, Mayer und Müller, 1924, vol. III, pp. 403–53. See also Giovanni Silvano, "Fichte e Machiavelli nella Prussia napoleonica," *Critica Storica* XXI (1984): 176–95.

22. Thomas Babington Macaulay, "Machiavelli," in *Critical and Miscellaneous Essays*, Boston, Weeks, Jordan, and Company, 1890, pp. 78–79.

23. Ibid., pp. 116 and 122.

24. Ibid., pp. 125–26.

25. Edgar Quinet, *Les Révolutions d'Italie*, in *Oeuvres d'Edgar Quinet*, Paris, Hachette, 1895, bk. II, pp. 3–4.

26. "L'exhortation au prince de delivrer l'Italie des barbares, Marseillaise du seizième siècle, cri de triomphe, dans lequel non pas l'écrivain, mais l'homme se démasque tout à coup avec ses colères amasses; harangue héroïque, qui aussi

éclatante que la trompette, absout Machiavelli du sentier infernal qu'il a pris pour arriver à ce dénoûment," p. 264.

27. Carlo Cattaneo too had serious reservations about Machiavelli. He praised Machiavelli's writing on the need for an Italian militia, but he also remarked that Machiavelli did not quite understand that the true source of the Swiss military might was their federal constitution. See Carlo Cattaneo, *Ugo Foscolo e l'Italia*, in *Scritti Filosofici, Letterari e Vari*, Florence, Sansoni, 1957, p. 557.

28. Giuseppe Mazzini, *Parigi. Indirizzo di Giuseppe Mazzini al governo provvisorio in nome dell'Associazione Nazionale Italiana* (March 22, 1848), in Carlo Cattaneo, *Tutte le opere*, Mondadori, Milan, 1974, vol. V, pp. 1355–57. Lamartine, a member of the French revolutionary government, responded that the only part of Lamartine's address he did not like were the words in praise of Machiavelli. Italian patriots, he remarked, should instead learn from a pure patriot like George Washington. *Risposta del Sig. De Lamartine, membro del governo provvisorio della Repubblica Francese a una delegazione dell'Associazione Nazionale Italiana per la rigenerazione dell'Italia, 28 marzo, 1848*, ibid., p. 2005.

29. Giuseppe Mazzini, *Alleanza repubblicana*, in *Scritti politici*, ed. Terenzio Grandi and Augusto Comba, Turin, UTET, 1972, p. 993.

30. Ibid.

31. With the power of the state, and with a leader, Machiavelli believed he could found the Italian nation, failing to realize that it was necessary also to "recreate the people, recreate thought, recreate man, the Roman man of whom he dreamed." Francesco De Sanctis, *Storia della letteratura italiana*, ed. Niccolò Gallo, Turin, Einaudi-Gallimard, 1996, pp. 480–81, 545; English translation by Francesco De Sanctis,

History of Italian Literature, ed. Joan Redfern, New York, Harcourt, 1931, pp. 547–48, 624–25.

32. Ibid., pp. 511–12; English translation, *History of Italian Literature,* pp. 584–85.

33. Pasquale Villari, *Niccolò Machiavelli e i suoi tempi;* English translation by Madame Linda Villari, *The Life and Times of Niccolò Machiavelli,* London, T. Fisher Unwin, 1892, vol. I, p. xix.

34. Ibid., vol. II, p. 549.

35. "The last chapter was, as it were, the synthesis and explanation of the whole work"; ibid., vol. II, pp. 195, 232.

36. Ibid., p. 195.

37. Ibid.

38. Ibid., p. 196. Only if we interpret Machiavelli's prince as a founder and redeemer, Villari noted in the conclusion of his work, can we understand and justify his immoral counsels:

> But when, completing his analysis, and cruel labour of vivisection, Machiavelli proceeds to draw his conclusions, then at last the practical side and real aim of his work are clearly seen. It is a question of achieving the unity of his Italian motherland and of delivering it from foreign rule. This was certainly the holiest of objects; but Machiavelli well knew that in the conditions in which Italy and Europe were then involved it would be impossible to achieve that object without recurring to the immoral means practiced by the statesmen of his time. Pursued by this idea, and dominated by this theme, Machiavelli did not pause to disentangle the scientific, general and permanent aim of his book from the practical aim and transitory means, apparently and, it may be, really essential to its achievement at that moment. It is needful, he said in the conclusion, to dare all things, and in view of the grandeur and sacredness of the end, to yield to

no scruples. Solely by the formation of a united, powerful, and independent nation can Italy acquire liberty, virtue and true morality. This is an enterprise only to be undertaken by a Prince–reformer, and by means suggested and imposed by history and experience. The people must afterwards complete and consolidate it by liberty, by national arms, by public and private virtue.

Ibid., p. 547.

39. Oreste Tommasini, *La vita e gli scritti di Niccolò Machiavelli nella loro relazione col machiavellismo*, Rome, Loescher, 1883–1911, vol. II, pp. 694 and 706. (I quote from the facsimile reprint, Bologna, Il Mulino, 1999.)

40. Lisio's words deserve to be quoted:

Nell'aver dunque colto dell'uomo le qualità tutte, permanenti attraverso i secoli; nell'aver disegnato con mano sicura la faccia e il cuore di quel fatale uomo che fu sempre il fondatore d'uno stato, d'una patria; nell'aver come determinato, eternandola nel *Principe*, l'energia individuale, e quanto possa su la società collettiva; in questo soltanto è riposta la ragion vera dell'immortalità del breve trattato. E la tragica figura si affaccia alla storia degli uomini in su l'aurora della civiltà: riappare più decisa, perché è più vicina a noi ne' fondatori delle monarchie nazionali di Europa: ci ha ultimamente commosso il cuore, quando sorse alfine chi volle e seppe redimere ed unire l'Italia. Così che, dovunque noi miriamo buono e forte stato, potenza e grandezza di nazione, agevole riesce scorgervi entro l'azione di uno, *Principe* anche di nome o soltanto di fatto.

I am quoting from the preface written in 1899; *Il Principe di Niccolò Machiavelli con commento storico, filologico e stilistico*, ed. Giuseppe Lisio, Florence, Sansoni, 1927, p. vi.

41. Ibid., p. x.
42. Ibid., p. xiv.
43. Benito Mussolini, "Preludio al Machiavelli," *Gerarchia* III (1924): 205–9.
44. Achille Norsa, *Il principio della forza nel pensiero politico di Machiavelli*, Milan, Ulrico Hoepli, 1936, pp. 35–38, 45.
45. Ibid., p. 46.
46. Ibid., p. 47.
47. Piero Gobetti, *La filosofia politica di Vittorio Alfieri*, in *Opere complete di Piero Gobetti*, vol. II, *Scritti storici, letterari e filosofici*, ed. Paolo Spriano, Turin, Einaudi, 1969, p. 126.
48. Piero Gobetti, *La rivoluzione liberale. Saggio sulla lotta politica in Italia*, in *Opere complete di Piero Gobetti*, vol. I, *Scritti politici*, ed. Paolo Spriano, Turin, Einaudi, pp. 923–24.
49. Federico Chabod, *Introduzione al "Principe,"* in *Scritti su Machiavelli*, Turin, Einaudi, 1993, p. 22; English translation by David Moore, *Machiavelli and the Renaissance*, London, Bowes & Bowes, 1958, p. 23.
50. Ibid, p. 22; English translation, p. 23.
51. Ibid., p. 27.
52. Ibid., p. 124.
53. Antonio Gramsci, *Quaderni del carcere*, ed. Valentino Gerratana, Turin, Einaudi, 2007, vol. III, p. 1555; English translation, *Selections from Prison Notebooks*, p. 316. Also Mario Martelli has stressed the outstanding value of Gramsci's interpretation of *The Prince*. See Mario Martelli, "Introduzione a Niccolò Machiavelli, *Il Principe*," *Edizione Nazionale delle Opere*, I, 1, ed. Mario Martelli, Rome, Salerno Editrice, 2006, pp. 47–48.
54. Gramsci, *Quaderni dal carcere*, vol. 3, p. 1555.
55. Ibid.
56. Ibid., p. 1556; English translation, pp. 328–29.
57. Ibid., p. 1556; English translation, p. 329.

58. Ibid., pp. 1617–18; English translation, 332–35.
59. Ibid., pp. 1600–1601.
60. Ibid., pp. 1577–78.
61. Augustin Renaudet, *Machiavelli*, 2nd ed., Paris, Gallimard, 1956, p. 28.
62. Ibid., p. 91.
63. Ibid., p. 9.
64. Luigi Russo, *Machiavelli*, 3rd ed., Bari, Laterza, 1949, p. 30.
65. Ibid., p. 8.

INDEX

Solon, 133
Statesman (Plato), 120
Strauss, Leo, 4–6

Theophrastus redivivus (anon.),
118
Theseus, 23, 26, 28*f*, 31–32,
114–15; greatness and nobility
of spirit of, 52; Machiavelli's
imagining of, 69
Tinkler, John F., 167n8, 170n29
Tommasini, Oreste, 134–35
Traité des trois imposteurs (unknown), 118–19

Uzano, Niccolò da, 50–51

Valentino. *See* Borgia, Cesare,
Duke Valentino
Vanini, Giulio Cesare, 119
Va' Pensiero (Verdi), 126

Vasari, Giorgio, 38*f*, 71*f*, 93*f*
Verdi, Giuseppe, 126
Vernacci, Giovanni, 62
Vesta journal, 124
Vettori, Francesco, 164n29; on
coherent interpretation of
politics, 164n29; encouragement of Machiavelli's writing,
64–65, 159n58; on international affairs, 87–88; Machiavelli's letters to, 29, 35–36, 58,
60–62, 155n14
Villari, Pasquale, 132–34,
175n38
*La vita e gli scritti di Niccolò Machiavelli nella loro relazione col
Machiavellismo* (Tommasini),
134–35

Walzer, Michael, 13–14
Wolin, Sheldon, 11–12